FLORISTS' REVIEW

one hundred one

HOW-TO
FAVORITES

PRESIDENT: Frances Dudley, AAF

PUBLISHER: Talmage McLaurin, AIFD

AUTHORS/EDITORS: Shelley Urban
David L. Coake
Kelsey E. Smith
Amy Bauer
Landon R. Hall

PHOTOGRAPHER: Stephen Smith

VISUAL EDITOR: James Miller, AIFD

ART DIRECTOR: Linda Lucero

FLORAL DESIGNERS: Talmage McLaurin, AIFD
Bill J. Harper, AIFD, AAF
Christina M. Burton, AIFD
James Miller, AIFD
Paula DeClerk
Patrick Wages
Tina Stoecker, AIFD, PFCI
Ann Jordan, AIFD, AAF, MMFD
Perry Walston, AIFD

Florists' Review is the only independent trade magazine for professional florists in the United States. In addition to serving the needs of retail florists through its monthly publication, the magazine has an active book division that supplies educational products to all who are interested in floral design. For more information, visit *Florists' Review's* Web site at *www.floristsreview.com* or call (800) 367-4708.

Florists' Review's 101 How-to Favorites Volume 2 was designed and produced by Florists' Review Enterprises, Inc., Topeka, Kansas. *www.floristsreview.com*

Printed in China by Oceanic Graphic Printing.

ISBN: 978-0-9714860-9-6

contents

bulb flowers 4

glass vase arrangements . . . 18

gourds 32

hearts 42

leaf tricks 58

nests 70

novelties 82

roses 96

sheaves 118

stems, twigs & vines 130

topiaries 146

wear & carry 156

wedding 170

wreaths & candle rings 190

index 206

1 Soak a block of colored floral foam until it is completely saturated. Scoop out balls of foam with a melon ball utensil.

2 Smooth the surface of the floral foam balls by rolling them between the palms of your hands, one at a time.

3 Arrange tulips in a bunch in your hand. Place the bunch to lean against one side of the vase. Drop in the foam balls around the stems to hold them in place.

Tulip Cocktail

An eye-catching gift with long-lasting added value.

Luscious lipstick-hued tulips, gathered into a showy bundle, are paired with colored floral foam in sweet watermelon-like balls that look juicy enough to eat. In addition to their unexpected and taste-tempting appearance, the hot-pink orbs support the tulip stems and maintain the blooms' jaunty post.

The materials are assembled inside a chic footed glass vessel that resembles a water goblet, making it ideal to contain the beverage-inspired arrangement. Moreover, when the tulips have faded, the vase remains as a useful gift as well since it may serve a variety of purposes, including that of pretty hurricane-style holder for a pillar candle.

Bulb Pot

A clay pot goes from common to cool with a faux aging technique.

Appearing wonderfully aged, as if it had been rescued from an old-fashioned potting shed, a brand new terra-cotta pot is transformed into a chic container with the help of an easy faux-finish paint treatment.

Once the quick-aging process is complete, the "weathered" vessel makes a grand container for mixed floral arrangements, especially those of classic gardeny blooms. Here, a mounded collection of tulips, *Gerberas* and *Freesias* mingles with foliages and clipped grasses, demonstrating the drama of the garden-flower and treated-pot pairing. These materials were selected, in part, for their striking tones, which cleverly repeat those of the painted pot.

1 Dip a clay pot into a container of water to thoroughly dampen the pot. This prevents the pot from overabsorbing paint.

2 Before applying paint, spray the pot with light mists of soapy water to produce moisture beads.

3 Spray the pot with whitewash paint, then with light coats of mossy green and basil paint. Alternate sprays of soapy water and all three paints until the desired look is achieved.

1 Place a stem of *Narcissus* against a *Galax* leaf, resting the flowers in the foliage's cleft.

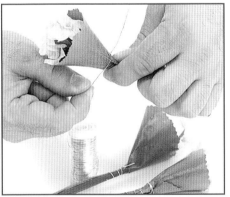

2 Wrap the *Galax* leaf around the *Narcissus* blossoms, and pierce a wire through the leaf to secure it in place. Wrap the wire around the stem.

3 Place all of the leaf-wrapped *Narcissus* stems together, and bind them in posy fashion with waterproof tape. Tie a ribbon around the binding point to conceal the tape.

Spring Notions

Convey romance with a hand-tied posy in a charming bud vase.

This bundle of fragrant polyanthus *Narcissi* (*N. tazetta* 'Paperwhite') makes a great drop-in accessory for bud vases and is especially striking in this organically shaped cool-blue selection.

The flowers' stems are individually wrapped with *Galax* leaves, which incorporates foliage into the design in an inventive manner and makes the diminutive white blooms significantly more pronounced and impacting.

A sheer, pale-blue ribbon, tied in a simple bow, accents the flowers' innocent beauty and conceals the waterproof tape that binds them. With its fresh blue, green and yellow hues, this composition is a great way to welcome spring.

Balanced Bulbs

Reinvent how bulb-flower lovers see their favorite flowers.

Bashful grape hyacinths *(Muscaris)* and sunny, diminutive polyanthus *Narcissi* are beloved springtime favorites, and connoisseurs of bulb flowers will gasp with excitement at this inventive design.

These casual clusters of delicate and intoxicatingly fragrant blossoms are combined with exotically gorgeous glory lilies *(Gloriosas)* and arranged inside salvaged amaryllis stems of varying lengths held erect in a shallow bowl on tiny kenzans (a.k.a. pin holders or pin frogs).

Filled with water, the hollow stems serve as ingenious organic vessels, and they elevate not only the height of the flowers but also the art of floral design. This daringly distinctive design can be adapted with any number of thin-stemmed flower types.

1 Secure pin holders, in assorted sizes, onto a ceramic plate or shallow bowl with floral clay.

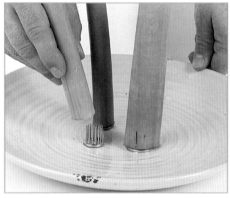

2 Select amaryllis stems in sizes to fit the pin holders. Carefully thread the hollow stems onto the pin holders.

3 Fill the basin of the plate or bowl with a shallow pool of water, and fill the amaryllis stems with water. Bundle the blossoms, and drop them into the stems.

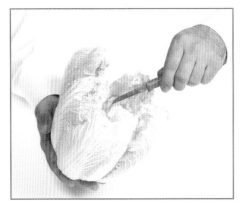

1 Gently loosen the leaves of a head of cabbage. Cut out the center of the cabbage to accommodate a container. Cut the bottom of the cabbage flat.

2 Place a liner or a container of choice into the center of the cabbage. Fill the container with properly mixed nutrient solution.

3 Arrange tulips in the container. If needed, fill the container with floral foam, or place a grid over the opening of the container before arranging the tulips.

Cabbage Patch

Leafy greens and fresh flowers fill an enticing menu.

Delightful as a centerpiece for a brunch or garden party, this casual arrangement of pale salmon-and-yellow-striped parrot tulips is created in a fresh Napa cabbage, which is hollowed out to accommodate a liner or a diminutive vase.

The pale green-and-white leaves of the Asian vegetable beautifully complement the soft colorations of the exquisite 'Salmon Parrot' tulips. Selections in bolder hues, from vibrant tangerine to even the deepest burgundies and fiery scarlets, would also "pop" from within the edible vessel.

The simple, gathered method of arranging these free-spirited blooms allows them to elongate and gracefully bow their beautiful heads as they will.

Garden Delight

Flowers and bulbs are placed to appear as if they are growing.

Arranged loosely among a few stems of goldenrod (*Solidago*) and real daffodil bulbs, purple *Irises* are just the thing to capture attention from nature-loving customers.

The weathered pot, which can be purchased as is or created with a faux finish technique (*see How-To 2 on Pages 6-7*), makes a perfect garden-style vessel for the materials. In addition, the floral foam, cut into a dome shape and covered with moss to resemble a mound of earth, creates a base from which the materials appear to sprout.

Customers who buy or receive this natural design get an extra treat with the bulbs, which can be planted after the fresh cut flowers fade.

1 Place wet floral foam to extend approximately 1 inch above the pot's rim. Using a knife, round the edges of the foam to create a dome shape.

2 Bend heavy-gauge wires into "U" shapes, and use them to secure moss to the foam. Greening pins provide another alternative for securing the moss to the foam.

3 Arrange *Irises* and *Solidago* into the center of the foam-filled pot. Secure daffodil bulbs to the moss-covered foam with wood picks.

1 Glue a piece of plastic foam into a clay rose pot, using hot-melt (pan) glue.

2 Insert a single tulip into the foam, and fill in around the tulip stem with gravel.

3 Brush rubber cement onto the rim of the pot, and attach a glass dome.

Topped Tulips

Glass domes distinguish simple permanent designs.

Cloches—bell-shaped glass covers—are traditionally used outdoors to protect plants from the elements. Here, cost-effective clochelike domes offer a different, purely decorative spin with single permanent tulips.

Each tulip stem is anchored into a dry- or plastic-foam-filled clay rose pot and surrounded by aquarium gravel or decorative rocks. Then, a simple clear glass dome is secured atop each pot.

This twist on a single flower presentation can be displayed individually or in multiples to add a touch of garden style to any room décor. And other single-bloomed springtime favorites, such as daffodils and hyacinths, can be presented under glass as well.

Zen Garden

Organic armatures support a bold mix of blooms.

Perched quietly atop a wooden base, a simple clear glass rose bowl becomes an Asian-inspired miniature water garden for those who value a modern aesthetic impacted by vibrant color harmony and textural intrigue.

The bowl is filled with polished stones and branchlets of curly willow, which serve as armatures to support the blooms— 'Bombay Gold' *Celosia* and three varieties of *Dahlias*. Their bold triadic color harmony and invitingly touchable textures make these flowers ideal for gift-giving or fresh home décor.

The concept of organic armatures inside an elevated rose bowl can be utilized with practically any blooms, especially those that are compact, textural and vividly hued.

1 Apply a strip of adhesive around the base of a rose bowl. Press the bowl onto a wooden stand to secure.

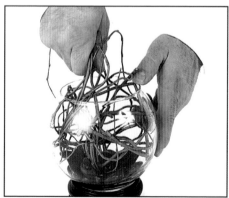

2 Fill the basin of the rose bowl with polished stones. Use enough stones to fill at least 1 inch, to camouflage the adhesive and support the flower stems.

3 Gather curly willow into a ball. Place it inside the rose bowl, and allow it to unfurl. Arrange flowers in a crisscross manner through the curly-willow armature.

1 Remove all foliage from carnation stems. In a hand-tied manner, gather the carnations into a nosegay.

2 Loosely arrange several bunches of lily grass into a vase. Place the carnation nosegay into the vase amid the lily grass.

3 Tuck the tips of the lily grass, several at a time, into the vase and carnation cluster to form random loops of greenery around and over the carnations.

Shining Stars

Radiant bicolor carnations shimmer among grassy loops.

This mounded gathering of bicolor carnations, whose petals are tipped with a striking white band, demonstrates the reinvigoration of this long-lasting flower that, thanks to new varieties and color combinations, is enjoying renewed popularity among consumers.

The carnations are complemented by looping blades of lily grass *(Liriope),* which position this design as a somewhat abstract offering.

Especially when each design incorporates carnations in different yet coordinating hues, these nosegays would be impacting in multiples. Given the tremendous array of carnations on the market, in both miniature and standard forms, a fantastic wealth of options is available.

Collared Vessel

A fresh garland adorns a basic bud vase in seasonal fashion.

Generally, there is nothing particularly wintry about *Gerberas*, but with a collar of cedar and two pine cones, the white flowers take on that seasonal ambience. For other seasons, similar custom treatments with different foliages can add flair to all kinds of simple vases.

For spring and summer, try collars of fresh herbs such as lavender or spiky plant materials such as heather, with freeze-dried or permanent fruits. Jeweled pins or baubles would be terrific additions, especially for gift-giving.

During autumn, fall leaves or textural vines adorned with nuts or faux gourds would accessorize autumn-hued *Gerberas* to complete delightful centerpieces. The possibilities for this technique are almost limitless.

1 Wrap decorative bullion wire around sprigs of cedar, joining them together to create a miniature garland of greenery.

2 Wrap the garland around the neck of the vase, leaving a length of bullion wire at one end to secure the ends of the garland together into a collar.

3 Hot-glue two small pine cones to the finished collar.

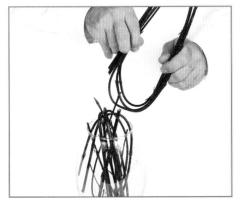

1 Bend red dogwood twigs into a "U" shape, and insert them into the vase facing various directions.

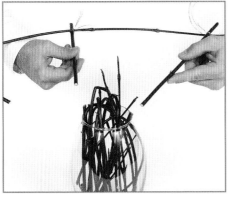

2 Wire three shorter twigs to one long twig with decorative wire. Insert the shorter twigs into the top of the design.

3 Anchor the longer twig with more twigs bent into an upside-down "U" shape. Finally, arrange flowers into the vase.

Stick It To 'em

Twigs in a variety of shapes and sizes form the base of this design.

Gladioli and vertical arrangement styles always have been staples of American floral design. But while this striking upright composition reminds us of floral traditions, its mechanics vary from the norm.

This design is anchored using a technique called *"kubari,"* an *Ikebana* term defined as "a mechanical support of straight, bent or forked twigs that sections or divides an upright container." The practice is used to form an attractive base for designs and could be used in several shapes of containers.

Here, branches of red dogwood *(Cornus)* are bent and twisted in various ways, performing both visual and structural functions since the branches support the stems of the *Gladioli* and croton leaves. The result is an updated and earthy retreat.

Floral Geometry

Round and square pair in this intriguing amaryllis arrangement.

With several blooms on each stem, these majestic amaryllises *(Hippeastrums)* appear to completely line the perimeter of the square glass container; however, as is evident inside the clear vessel, just a few stems are secured into the corners.

In contrast to the square form of the vase, a vine orb is dropped into the center. Clipped amaryllis stems, some decorated with beads and others with bands of copper bullion wire, form intriguing vertical lines. Meanwhile, Asian honeysuckle, swirled amid the massive blooms, repeats the circular dynamic created by the vine orb.

Keep just a small amount of water inside the vase because deep water may affect the orb's structure. Regular additions of water may be required.

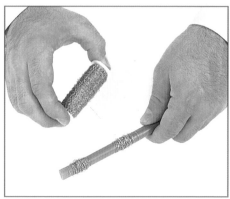

1 Apply a strip of clear tape about 1 inch from each side of a square vase. When the four strips are completed, small squares will be formed in each corner.

2 Apply decorative bands of copper bullion wire to salvaged amaryllis stems. Insert teardrop jewels into the ends of other stems.

3 Pour about 1 inch of water into the square vessel, drop the vine orb into the center, and insert one or two amaryllises into each corner. Add decorated amaryllis stems.

Fruited Tree

1 Tie a series of individual *Camellia* leaves onto a length of beading wire a few inches apart. Then, wrap the beading wire around the neck of the vase.

2 Thread a length of beading wire through several whole and half key limes. Wrap the fruit-laden wire around the neck of the vase, as well.

3 Arrange branches of *Camellia* foliage in the vase, and tie a few more key limes to them with beading wire. Before adding flowers, drop a few key limes into the vase.

Combined flowers and fresh fruits look good enough to eat.

Eye-catching miniature *Gerberas*, in a cheerful, sunny hue, form the focal point of this taste-tempting arrangement, but key limes are the key to its refreshingly delightful appeal.

Attached with beading wire to branches of *Camellia* foliage, the small citrus fruits appear to be growing in a miniature tree. Under water, sliced and whole key limes enliven the clear vase presentation, and additional key limes and clusters of immature grapes, both on beading wire, encircle the vase's neck.

This creative composition is wonderful for many sentiments and occasions, and its affordability ensures that it can be used in multiples, making the flowering fruit tree perfect for parties year-round, particularly when seasonal fruits are selected.

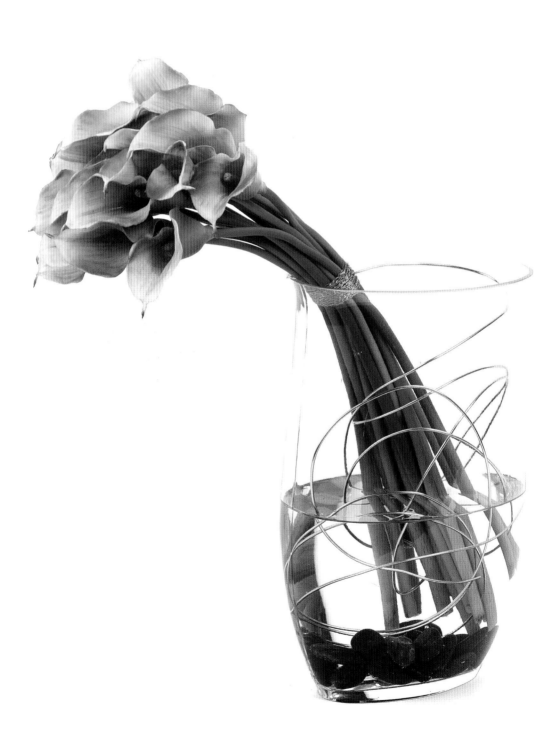

30 Glass Vase Arrangements

Bound Beauties

Colorful decorative wires direct free-form permanent callas.

For years, graceful callas have been placed into containers with their natural curves dictating the shapes of the arrangements. With these permanent callas, a more structured approach is taken. By binding the stems first with waterproof tape, then with colorful wire, they are formed into a tight but natural configuration as they cascade over the side of the vase for a decidedly asymmetrical composition.

Heavier-gauge decorative wire in a corresponding color is wound into large loops and placed into the vase after the container is filled with acrylic water, which keeps everything in place and adds realism to the display. Aerosol fabric protector comes in handy to seal the permanent stems and prevent their colors from bleeding into the acrylic water.

1 Spray the permanent calla stems with an aerosol fabric protector to keep the color from bleeding into the acrylic water.

2 Place washed and dried river rocks into the container. Following the manufacturer's instructions, prepare the acrylic water. Mix with a plastic utensil.

3 Secure the calla bundle in its desired position with waterproof tape until the faux water hardens. Once the solution is solid, remove the tape.

1. Glue wood picks into the bases of eight permanent gourds, and arrange the gourds into a foam-filled basket in two parallel rows.

2. Add auxiliary materials, such as permanent foliages, grasses and dried quince slices, around the bases of the gourds in a haphazardly appearing manner.

3. Clip straw into small bits, and sprinkle it atop the gourds and other materials in the basket. For added security, the straw can be glued in place.

Bountiful Basket

Permanent gourds and other seasonals fill a basket to overflowing.

Two parallel rows of permanent pear-shaped ornamentals, placed inside a rectangular gathering basket in an orderly manner, would form strong contemporary lines if not for the disorderly mass of permanent and dried leaves, grasses and quince slices tucked around the gourds. Clipped bits of straw also are sprinkled atop the composition, further enhancing the unkempt appearance of the accent materials, which together soften the strong lines and make the design more casual, comfortable and inviting.

This modern design also is achievable with fresh gourds and other seasonal staples, but since these permanent and dried options are equally affordable and longer-lasting, this design can decorate the home or office throughout an entire season.

Nature's Vase

Dried gourds make delightful containers for arrangements.

A large bottle gourd with its top removed and its bottom filed flat, so it will stand upright, is the perfect vessel for a collection of lasting botanicals, including dried quince slices and small gourds as well as permanent safflowers *(Carthamus),* berries and leaves.

Most of the materials are arranged into the dry foam that fills the freeze-dried vessel, but their arrangement is given abstract flair with the crisscrossing lines of mahogany-stained river cane and pale stems reserved from other projects.

Capture attention by presenting multiple versions of this design, especially in different sizes using a mix of smaller gourds. They'll have tremendous impact wherever they're displayed.

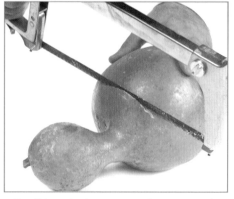

1 Using a hacksaw, remove the narrow end, or neck, of a large freeze-dried gourd.

2 File the base of the gourd flat so it will stand upright. Glue dry foam into the gourd with hot-melt (pan) glue.

3 Arrange permanent and dried florals into the foam. Hot glue river cane into the floral mass, forming a crisscross pattern.

1 Gently pull on the sides of a pine-straw nest to loosen and enlarge it. Then, secure the nest atop a dry-foam-filled pot with Dixon pins.

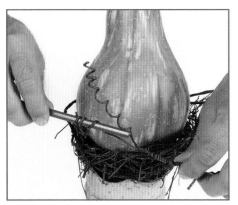

2 Glue two wood picks into the base of a permanent gourd, and place the gourd inside the nest, inserting the wood picks into the dry foam.

3 Wrap a length of permanent vine around the nest. Curl the loose ends around a pencil to form decorative "tendrils."

Nested Fruits

Quick crafts and ready-made accessories pair for maximum impact.

Welcome seasonal colors and textures with small permanent accessory items, such as ready-made gourd-covered candlesticks and a trio of gourd-topped pots. They and other similar fruited designs will have unlimited appeal and multiple applications at a modest price.

The candlesticks can be purchased as shown, and creating the small pots requires only pine-straw nests, which are wrapped with permanent vines and form organic "thickets" atop which the gourds are nestled. The nests are simply affixed atop dry-foam-filled vintage-inspired iron pots, and the gourds are secured into the foam with wood picks.

The ease of creating this ornamental spread only enhances its appeal, as does its attractive price.

Two Towers

Permanent gourds create imaginative topiarylike spires.

Resembling small, organic totem poles, these towers of gourds are an inventive way to showcase permanent fruits. Look for dramatic shapes and styles, and mix colors as needed to enhance the décor of the pieces' intended destination.

Interspersed among these permanent gourds, which are threaded onto a river-cane pole, are several preserved salal leaves. Their curled edges—the more curly the better—provide a necessary and eye-catching contrast between each of the intriguing ornamentals.

A specialized paint treatment, alternating sprays of moss-green paint and soapy water, gives the pots a realistic aged appearance and repeats the nature-inspired greens in the fruitful spires.

1 Faux-age a clay pot with alternating sprays of green paint and soapy water. Fill the pot with dry foam, and insert a river cane pole into the center of the foam.

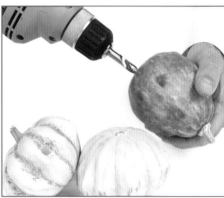

2 Drill holes through each of several permanent gourds, so they may be skewered onto the river cane pole.

3 Cut small holes in the salal leaves, and thread the leaves onto the pole in groupings. Add a gourd, and continue alternating leaves and gourds to reach the desired height.

1 Clean the exterior of a cylinder vase with glass cleaner to remove any oily residues.

2 Adhere long, narrow gourds all around the exterior of the vase with hot-melt (pan) glue.

3 Glue several small tufts of reindeer moss between each of the gourds, to fill in the gaps.

Botanical Cylinder

Permanent gourds gloriously disguise a cylinder vase.

Long, narrow gourds, which somewhat resemble their cucumber cousins, are affixed with pan glue to the exterior of a cylinder vase, transforming an inexpensive container into a fabulous receptacle for all types of seasonal blossoms. Between each of the vertically placed permanents, tufts of reindeer moss not only fill space but lend an uncultivated and appropriately organic texture.

The gourds' slightly curving necks and curling stems add drama to the easy-to-make design, and their neutral hues afford unlimited color possibilities in the fresh flower selection. Since the container can be reused, consumers can replace faded blooms regularly to have a continuously fresh decorative accessory to brighten their kitchens and dining areas.

Idyllic Planting

A bloom-covered form conveys the serenity of a field of wildflowers.

Resembling a patch of wild blossoms that have unexpectedly sprouted across a grassy hillside, individual hybrid *Delphinium* blooms are arranged atop a lush bed of bells-of-Ireland to create this design.

While it may appear labor intensive, covering the heart form is actually quick work. When the bell-shaped florets are cut into sections and pressed into the saturated floral foam, each cluster covers several inches of surface area.

Atop the bells-of-Ireland placements, a scattering of *Delphinium* florets is inserted into the foam and secured with black-headed corsage pins. The flowers are placed in a haphazard manner, and three varieties of *Delphiniums*, in lavender, blue and purple, are used, enabling the design to closely resemble nature's handiwork.

1 Cut stems of bells-of-Ireland above each cluster of blooms, leaving stems long enough to insert into the floral foam.

2 Arrange each cluster into the floral foam until the entire surface of the heart is covered.

3 Insert *Delphinium* florets throughout the "field" of bells-of-Ireland using black-headed corsage pins to secure the blooms.

Ribbon Accents

Wired-ribbon hearts accessorize an updated Victorian bouquet.

1 Spray-paint a clay pot to match the colors of the flowers in your design.

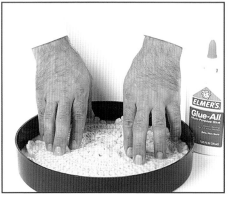

2 Soak a doily in a mixture that is 50 percent white glue and 50 percent water.

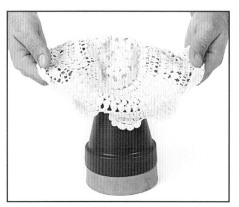

3 Invert and elevate the painted pot, and lay the doily over it. Shape the doily to the pot so that it will extend slightly above the rim when the pot is upright.

The tussie-mussie, a diminutive, aromatic nosegay of flowers, is a traditional bouquet that has been around since Europe's medieval times. The small nosegays were made primarily of scented medicinal herbs that were believed to ward off the plague. But it wasn't until Queen Victoria's time that the language of flowers reached its prime and gentlemen began communicating feelings by sending private and intimate messages to ladies by means of these special bouquets.

This design transforms the tradition of romantic posies with lace edging into a delightful arrangement that mimics the old-fashioned idea. Several hearts made of wired ribbon contribute to the vintage feel and add dimension to the mini mound. The painted clay pot is covered with a doily, so the Victorian feel is maintained.

Beaded Bouquet

Handcrafted accents glamorize a grand group of roses.

With their exquisite scarlet and powdery-white petals, a quintet of gorgeous 'Latin Lady' roses are the showpieces of this modest-scale design. Yet the glitzy, low-cost beaded accents somehow manage to enhance the roses' glamorous appeal, as do the sprigs of tree fern, which seem to imitate a luxurious feathery boa.

The beaded accents, one of which is shaped into a glimmering bejeweled heart, are quickly custom crafted from inexpensive plastic beads or recycled Christmas ornaments and garland. Then they're simply tucked among the blooms.

The modern ceramic vessel, selected to match the colors of the jeweled accessories, is the ideal complement for this affordable yet high-style arrangement.

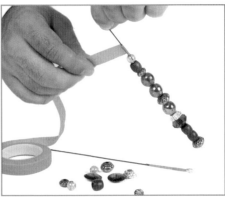

1 Tape pearl-headed corsage pins onto one end of several pieces of heavy-gauge wire.

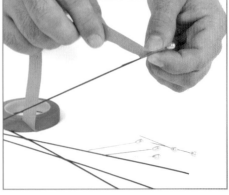

2 String beads onto the wires, then apply stem wrap to the ends of the wires to hold the beads in place.

3 Shape one of the bead-covered wires into a heart. Tape the heart onto a wood pick.

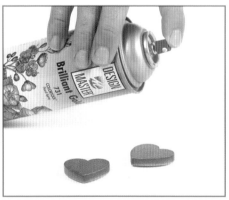

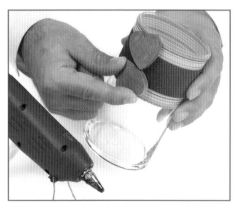

1 Secure woven ribbon just beneath a cylinder vase's rim with spray adhesive. Apply a narrower velvet ribbon atop the woven ribbon with spray adhesive.

2 Spray gold paint onto both sides of two wooden craft hearts.

3 Hot-glue the painted hearts atop the ribbon, disguising the seams.

Heartfelt Expression

Painted wooden hearts add value to simple cylinder-vase designs.

Serving as a customized alternative to the traditional three-rose bud vase, a mix of rose varieties, including 'Latin Lady' and 'Sweet Unique,' offers increased visual interest over single varieties of roses.

The rosy groupings are displayed in basic cylinders along with a few stems of *Nerines* and *Ruscus*. The vessels are customized with strips of elegant woven ribbon overlaid with hot-pink velvet ribbon, which are adhered with spray adhesive. The result is tailored bandings that add tremendous perceived value to the compositions.

Covering the seams of the bandings, gold-painted wooden hearts playfully embellish the ribbon, imparting a stylish and feminine belt-buckle feel to the vases.

Botanical Ardor

An organically covered heart highlights roses "planted" in grass.

By carefully positioning the blades of lily grass—some vertical and some horizontal but all with their ends in the saturated floral foam—an intriguing abstract structure is formed. Although the vibrant red roses also are arranged into the foam, the blooms appear to be laid upon the grassy formation, and the resulting complementary color harmony gives the flowers a truly show-stopping appeal.

Continuing that dramatic complementary palette, a heart cut from crimson felt is adhered to cardboard and accessorized with bits of raffia and snipped blades of lily grass. The modern accent is attached near the rim of the ceramic planter and seamlessly unites the fresh 'Opium' roses and their neutral-toned container.

1 Trace a heart pattern onto cardboard, and cut out the cardboard heart. Cut another heart out of red felt.

2 Adhere the felt heart to the cardboard heart with spray adhesive. Apply short strips of lily grass and raffia onto the felt, also with spray adhesive.

3 Hot-glue the decorated heart onto the exterior of the container.

1. Trace any size heart pattern onto a piece of thick cardboard or foam-centered board, and cut it out.

2. Spray the heart form with dark green paint, and let it dry. Then spray it with adhesive, and wait for it to get "tacky."

3. Lay short pieces of *Equisetum* onto the sticky heart-shaped form, and let dry. Then trim the *Equisetum* into a heart shape following the pattern.

Reed Heart

Give a creative twist to a traditional mass composition.

For practically any occasion for which loving sentiments need to be expressed, consider this pretty, symmetrical mass arrangement, with radial rhythm. Through the pairing of lots of spikes of larkspurs and miniature carnations, along with the moss-encrusted ceramic container into which the materials are arranged, this affectionate design offers romantics a natural, gardeny casualness.

Enhancing the sense of nature-inspired amour is a custom-designed but quick-to-make heart-shaped insert. The *Equisetum*-covered accent says "I love you" in a simple, organic manner, and it has an enchanting panache that no manufactured plastic pick can match.

Modern Heart Picks

Contemporary treatments distinguish gatherings of roses.

Featuring bold splashes of red 'Charlotte' roses, this pair of simple rose arrangements rises to whatever the romantic occasion with modern flair that is accomplished through the use of handmade Japanese papers and silver wired cording.

The thin black paper, which is secured using floral adhesive, lends textural interest through a layered effect. And because it is transparent in several spots, it resembles a sophisticated lacy treatment.

Silver wired cording is formed into two modern heart shapes that extend above each vase, and the covered wire also forms "tails" onto which beads are threaded on the smaller vase. Acrylic pebbles add further dimension at the bottoms of the vases.

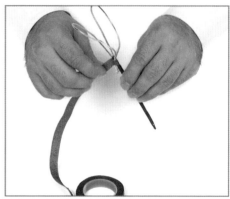

1 Cut two equal-length pieces of stiff, narrow wired cording.

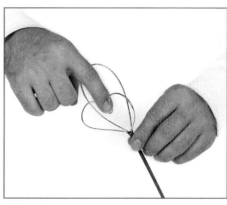

2 Gather the four ends together to form two teardrop shapes. Attach them to a wired wood pick, and cover with stem wrap.

3 Indent the center of each teardrop shape with your finger until a heart shape is created.

1 Cut equal-sized squares of burlap and cellophane. Place the cellophane atop the burlap. Wrap the squares around the pot, and tie with raffia, ribbon or twine.

2 Spray appropriately sized wooden craft hearts with paint to coordinate or contrast with the plant.

3 Attach the painted hearts to the burlap wrapping with double-sided tape.

Amorous Azaleas

Easy treatments dress up plants for romantic gift-giving.

In just three simple steps, you can increase a plant's perceived value while adding a personal design and creative touch that will make your offerings stand out from the crowd. It also will enable your planted merchandise to send sentiments of love for all romantic occasions.

Simply cover a grower's pot with layers of cellophane, to prevent leakage, and burlap. Wooden craft hearts, painted to match or contrast with the colors of your chosen plant, delightfully accessorize the covering. Double-sided tape is an easy mechanic for adhering the hearts to the burlap.

This simple and attractive upgrade is appropriate for all types of blooming and foliage plants.

Tropical Feasting

Brightly-hued tropical leaves complement a warm-toned centerpiece.

A gardeny mix of safflowers, butterfly weed and black-eyed Susans takes an exotic turn with the addition of yellow kangaroo paws and broad croton leaves, which are used to cover the low-cost papier-mâché pot. The leaves' naturally varying hues extend the composition's color harmony to the container, where the tropical gold, orange and green foliage adds an intriguing visual element.

The grand centerpiece will take center stage, and if complementary arrangements are needed for lengthy buffets and tables, consider tiny bud vases, each enwrapped with a single croton leaf, filled with just a few safflowers, butterfly weed and black-eyed Susans.

1 Carefully cut off the flared rim of a papier-mâché pot with a sharp knife, and fill the pot with saturated floral foam.

2 Cut the bases of croton leaves straight, to be flush with the pot's bottom. Make sure the leaves are long enough to conceal the pot's cut rim.

3 Spray adhesive onto the backsides of the croton leaves, and press the leaves onto the pot in an overlapping manner.

1 Spray the front sides of a handful of salal leaves with adhesive.

2 Spray the back sides of another handful of leaves with adhesive.

3 Press the leaves onto the rim of the basket, irregularly alternating between front sides and back sides.

Bright Basket

This leaf-collared basket supports an uplifting design.

This cheery arrangement is composed of warm, bright hues and touchable textures. The materials, including orange *Gerberas*, yellow miniature callas, sunflowers, pincushions *(Leucospermums)* and more, are arranged in a traditional wooden slat basket that has a flat-sided rim. To make a comfortable segue between the basket and the flowers, the rim is covered with salal leaves that are adhered in what appears to be a random manner. The resulting leafy collar, with casual, haphazard charm, contributes to the arrangement's happy mood.

Throughout the year, consumers can give it as a gift or use it to decorate a setting in need of radiance and cheer.

Radiant Rows

Slender vases highlight intriguing foliages and gorgeous golden roses.

Within the clean, contemporary lines of these narrow pocket vases, eye-catching foliage transforms quartets of roses into works of art.

In the foreground, diminutive 'Yellow Folies' spray roses, all clipped from a single stem, are nestled into a watery bed of captivating 'Milky Way' *Aspidistra* foliage, which features starry speckles on its intensely green leaves.

In the background, a more substantial yet still slender vessel holds luminous 'Yellow Coral' hybrid tea roses that gleam amid variegated *Aspidistra* leaves, whose creamy stripes repeat the flowers' sunny hues.

In both compositions, blades of lily grass, some of which are inverted so their white tips are visible, complete the modern aesthetic.

1 Fold variegated *Aspidistra* leaves in half, and insert the folded ends into a pocket vase.

2 Position the roses and lily grass stems (some with their white tips up) into the vase, with stems inside the folded-leaf pockets.

3 Fold down the pointed tips of the 'Milky Way' *Aspidistra* foliage, and tuck them into the vase. Wedge a lime slice between the outer leaves and the vase wall.

1 Apply spray adhesive to the back sides of stemless *Galax* leaves, and press them onto the exterior of the basket in a random overlapping pattern.

2 Where the handle joins the basket, insert lily grass into the floral foam on both sides, and position it up and over the handle. Secure with wire at the top and at both sides.

3 Insert two more stems of lily grass into the foam, one on each side, and coil them around the handle to cover the wire and add a decorative touch.

Perfect Harmony

Leaves, grasses and flowers form a nature-inspired union.

Curling blades of lily grass *(Liriope)* swirl gracefully around this baskets' grass-covered handle while overlapping *Galax* leaves organically conceal the woven basin. Inside, an exquisite botanical gathering is completed with bicolor 'Ambiance' roses and 'Tundra' carnations, which combine with golden 'Honey Flair' *Hypericum*. Additional *Galax* leaves, rolled into conical forms, add volume, texture and a novel design element.

This glorious organic basket will make a delightful gift for all types of occasions and holidays. And just envision multitudes of them topping tables at a sophisticated garden party or outdoor wedding reception.

Gladly Magnificent

Tall, bold *Gladioli* make this arrangement stand up and stand out.

Perfect for any kind of formal setting or even as a sympathy tribute, the strong lines of this design draw lots of attention. And though it has a complex appearance, this piece is quite simple to assemble.

With the strong, columnar placement of *Gladioli*, a stately vertical form is created. *Calathea* leaves are arranged in a variety of configurations—natural, rolled and even fanned—to add horizontal dimension and interest to the design. The finished shape is almost triangular, being both boldly vertical and horizontal.

Although the mixture of traditional *Gladioli* and exotic *Calathea* leaves is an eclectic pairing, it works well and provides a showy, upscale piece that would be at home in a variety of proper settings.

1 Begin the design by arranging *Gladioli* into a columnar form in the vase.

2 Add leaves to the design to expand the form of the column. Create looped leaves by poking a hole in each leaf, curling it and putting the stem through the hole.

3 Create a center leaf "fan" by bunching the leaf into a fan shape, stapling it and using it instead of a bow.

1 Arrange *Alstroemerias* in your hand, and place the cluster into a mint-julep cup.

Leave It to Red

Satin corsage leaves bedeck a casual cluster of *Alstroemerias*.

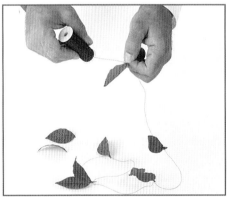

2 Wrap bullion wire around the ends of permanent leaves, a few times around each, to create a garland.

3 Wrap the leaf garland around the bouquet, tucking the wire and leaves securely among the blooms.

Dressed up with a few accessories, this simple nosegay begins with several stems of *Alstroemerias* that are clustered at the same height to create the perfect shape. Pine cones are picked into the design, adding a wintry touch to the blossoms.

The striking scarlet leaves, which appear tucked into the blooms, are actually satin corsage leaves that are strung on shimmering red bullion wire. The resulting custom-crafted garland enwraps the *Alstroemeria* grouping and adds punches of color among the botanicals, carrying the color of the mint-julep cup to the design it holds. Finishing the color story is a modern wide mesh ribbonlike treatment.

Select wires and leaves in varying colors to adapt this concept to any occasion.

Heather Nest

Filler flowers compose an easy-to-assemble novelty.

Fashioned from fresh heather that is assembled into a "garland" with gold beading wire, this flowery nest makes a soft, cozy spot in which to nestle wooden eggs. The faux eggs are colored with various hues of spray paint to achieve the natural mottled effect.

Use this charming creation in multiples to decorate tables at all types of affairs, from small, casual brunches to grand gatherings.

Although it will become somewhat fragile as the heather dries, this nest can become as long-lasting as it is lovely with a few sprays of an aerosol sealant or light adhesive. And any shed blooms can simply be gathered and sprinkled into the center.

1 Wire several stems of heather end to end, in garland fashion, with gold beading wire, to create a long strip of heather.

2 Break or snap (by bending) the woody stems of the heather garland about every inch or so.

3 Coil the "articulated" garland to form a nest, starting with the bottom of the nest. Stitch the coils, where needed, with beading wire, so the nest will hold its shape.

Grass Nest

Clipped grasses are glued into a realistic avian abode.

1 Spray the inside of a disposable container with aerosol leaf shine to prevent the bear-grass clippings from sticking to the container. Clip grasses into 1-inch-long pieces.

Resembling the real home-building handiwork of its intended occupant, this nest is made entirely of bear-grass clippings that are held together with a little spray adhesive. The glued grasses are formed by hand to replicate a newly assembled bird sanctuary.

2 Sprinkle grass clippings into the container, and spray them with adhesive. Shake the container, and spray again. Repeat this process until a sticky pile of clippings results.

Inspired by a remote woodlands lodge outfitted with a luxurious down-filled bed, the interior of the natural-looking nest is lined with fluffy feathers to create a warm place in which a collection of natural quail eggs is incubated.

The nest's realistic appearance lends it to a wealth of organic applications. Throughout the year, tuck it into woodsy floral arrangements, permanent trees and other compositions that will benefit from a natural accent.

3 Spray your finger tips with aerosol leaf shine, and form the mass of bear-grass pieces into a "nest." While the adhesive is slightly tacky, line the nest with feathers.

Vine Nest

Wild-looking nito vine closely replicates a natural structure.

A natural and befitting medium, a clump of nito vine provides an easy solution for creating custom-made nests. And to help the handmade bird habitats hold their shapes, the nito vine formation is permanently set with a mixture of white glue and water.

And to give it a realism that, heretofore, only a bird could create, the exterior of the nest is wrapped with other natural materials—adhesive-coated strands of raffia and blades of bear grass.

Set in a place of honor upon a stone urn, this feather-lined version, filled with a half-dozen quail eggs, resembles a found nest that was blown from its tree by strong breezes and plucked from the ground by an attentive passer-by.

1 Mix equal parts of white glue and water in a mixing bowl. Dip a mass of nito vine into the glue/water mixture.

2 Place the saturated vine into a metal bowl, and press it into a nest shape. Let it air-dry, or place it into a low-temp oven to dry faster.

3 Remove the dry vine nest from the bowl. Spray a few strands of raffia and pieces of bear grass with adhesive, and randomly wrap them around the outside of the nest.

Twig Nest

1 Wrap beading wire around the middle of 1-inch-long twigs. After wrapping each twig, twist the wire once before adding the next twig. Space the twigs about 1/2 inch apart.

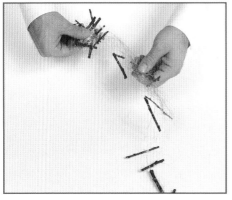

2 Wind angel hair into one end of twig garland. Coil that end to form the nest's base. Add angel hair to the next section, and continue coiling. Repeat until the nest is sized right.

3 Form a wad of angel hair into a nest shape to fit inside the twigs. Press it into the nest to form a gold lining. Paint several acorns gold, and place them into the nest along with feathers.

A glittering, 14-karat home is crafted for a layer of golden eggs.

Constructed of inch-long birch and pussy-willow twigs, which are strung closely together in garland fashion with gold beading wire, this "gilty" nest is opulently woven with golden angel hair, making it a palatial home suitable for the finest feathered creatures.

Although the only things they could possibly hatch are goldcup oak trees, glitzy gold-painted acorns are novel substitutes for faux or real eggs. This swanky option is a dazzling accent applicable for even the most glamorous occasions. Nestle it amid branches and into fashionable faux or fresh wreaths or wherever else such a striking accessory is called for.

Plant Enhancer

Resembling straw, a raffia nest accessorizes seasonal plant ware.

The exotic blossoms of orchid plants, like these spectacular violet-colored *Phalaenopsis*, are entrancing American consumers in record numbers. In fact, millions of potted orchids are sold in the United States each year, and the numbers are steadily growing.

The foliar portions of these tropical beauties, however, leave some customers wanting more. For them, orchid planters enhanced with other plant materials and accessories should fill the bill.

In the foreground, a raffia bird's nest filled with painted wooden eggs adds interest to the base of the orchid while bird's-nest ferns *(Aspleniums)* and a pink-and-green variegated polka-dot plant *(Hypoestes)* accentuate the other potted beauties.

1 Cut raffia into 1-inch-long pieces, and place them into a shallow disposable container.

2 Spray the raffia pieces with adhesive and shake them around in the container until they stick together in a ball-like clump.

3 After the adhesive starts to dry but while it is still tacky, form the mass of raffia into a "nest." Once the desired shape is achieved, spray it with adhesive a final time, and let it dry.

1 Layer twigs of deciduous huckleberry atop a scented geranium leaf to begin forming a nest.

2 Wrap the leaf and twigs with green bullion wire, both vertically and horizontally, forming the nest shape.

3 Pierce the nest with a lilac branch, and insert the branch into the arrangement. Add a small egg to the nest with hot glue.

Nestled In

A nest made from common design-table ingredients.

While ready-made nests are time-efficient, this nest is as well, being quickly crafted from a scented geranium leaf and sprigs of deciduous huckleberry bound with bullion wire.

A slender galvanized watering can accompanies this fragrant bouquet, which is arranged in a clear cylinder vase. The vase is set inside the watering can to avoid any interaction between the metal and the flower-food solution and to protect the container from rust.

A variety of colors and forms are incorporated to give this arrangement a natural and balanced harmony. From lilacs and peonies to a bit of evergreen pine, the bouquet conveys nature's exquisite abundance.

Seeing Spots

Cool customized treatments revamp a potted bloomer.

Potted *Gerberas* are hip selections for self-purchase or gift-giving. To dress them up a bit, drop the original grower pot inside a clay or ceramic pot, such as this crisp, white-washed version.

A playful polka-dot ribbon, which is hot-glued and casually tied around the painted pot's rim, is the perfect retro embellishment for such a chic potted plant. The wired ribbons' rolled ends—done by wrapping the ribbon around a pencil—adds a stylish finishing touch.

But what really completes the package is the pretty spotted butterfly, fashioned from the same dotted ribbon. It complements the plant's cheery demeanor at little additional cost.

1 Cut two pieces of ribbon, one slightly larger than the other, into the shape of adhesive bandages.

2 Place the two pieces together lengthwise, with the centers aligned. Scrunch them together in the center, and fasten them with a chenille stem.

3 Shape the ends of the chenille stems to resemble antennae, and hot glue a piece of leather lacing on the center to form the body.

Young Love

A sweet gift sends love to parents and children alike.

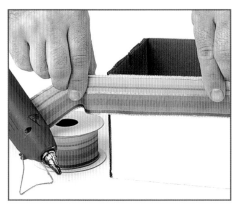

1 Hot-glue a strip of colorful ribbon around the topmost portion of a cardboard delivery box.

2 Select crayons randomly, and hot-glue them uniformly around the perimeter of the box.

3 Cover the interior of the box with polyfoil to protect the box from spillage. Place a foam-filled plastic liner inside the polyfoil-lined box, and arrange flowers.

Adhered in random order, colorful crayons affordably customize the exterior of a square delivery box to create a fanciful vessel for youngsters' expressions of love. Such an adorably loving sentiment will be well-received on Mother's Day, birthdays and other special celebrations as well as by children in hospitals. Inside the crayon-covered box, a cheery mix of flowers, including *Gerberas*, *Dahlias*, *Asters*, lilies, tulips and much more, is assembled from assorted or excess product, since any combination of hues will coordinate with the colorful container.

Handwritten sentiments lend childlike charm. Original works of art, created by pint-size "Picassos," would have similar whimsical appeal.

Funny Bunny

Cutesy "cottontail" creation imparts childlike cheer.

This adorable bunny design can serve as both a gift for kids and one that is given by kids to parents, grandparents, teachers and other beloved family and friends.

Its construction is almost simple enough for kids to do themselves, but most likely a little adult supervision and assistance will be required. Despite that the flexible straw basket's lid is secured in place with adhesive dots, the casual tie of ribbon adds stability as well as a handsome necktie for the google-eyed carnation hare.

A plastic bowl inside the basket, filled with floral foam, provides a water source for the foliages and the fluffy standard carnation, which is easily bedecked with fun facial features and chenille-stem ears.

1 Adhere the basket's lid to its base with adhesive dots. Place a foam-filled plastic bowl inside the basket. Arrange *Galax* and salal leaves, and secure with a casual tie of ribbon.

2 Bend chenille stems to form ears. Tape the ends together with floral tape. Apply floral adhesive to the taped end, and insert it into the carnation, between the petals and the calyx.

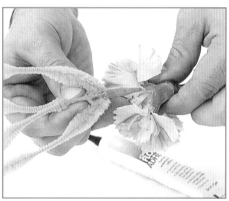

3 Insert the carnation into the foam-filled bowl, positioned so the bloom rests atop the bow. Apply google eyes, nose and raffia whiskers with floral adhesive.

1 Brush a mixture of equal parts water and white glue onto a bubble bowl. Apply squares of tissue paper, covering the bowl's surface. Brush the glue mixture over the paper.

2 Create a template for your spooky shape, such as this bat, out of kraft paper. Place the template onto craft foam, and cut around it.

3 Using adhesive dots, secure the foam shape to the inside of the bubble bowl. Make sure the bowl is large enough to keep the shape safely away from the votives' flames.

Batty Beauty

Spooky accessories repurpose elegant florals with fright value.

Incorporating an eerie orb that casts the ominous glow of flickering bat shadows, this design provides a novel twist on a traditional candle-ring arrangement.

The orb is simply a large bubble bowl opaquely covered with tissue, adhered with a mixture of equal parts water and white glue. (The covering can be removed with warm water.) Inside the bowl, which rests atop a floral-foam-filled tray in which the florals are arranged, four votive candles highlight the outlines of the frightening craft-foam bats.

Goldenrod (*Solidago*) that is painted black, along with large loops of plastic gutter covering, add chillingly dark touches among the gorgeous 'Star 2000' roses and salal leaves.

Crazy Candelabrum

Create a frightful decorative with edible accents.

Delightfully eerie yet magically delicious, this centerpiece, complete with hauntingly off-kilter candleholders anchored in plastic foam disguised by chocolate wafer "dirt," is a perfect accent for a party where spooky treats are being served. (Just remember to protect the surface beneath the candelabrum from the dripping wax.)

Creepy chenille spiders "crawl" up webs of black mesh that are fastened, along with a draping string of candy corn, to the long wooden stems of the candleholders. In addition, gooey gummy worms appear to be slithering from within.

With the wealth of other eerie edibles typically on the market around Halloween, similar seasonal decoratives can easily take an even more gruesome turn, if desired.

1 Pierce candy corn pieces with a corsage pin, and string them onto decorative wire that is knotted at the end.

2 Drill a hole into the center of a small clay pot, and insert a wooden candleholder, securing it with hot glue.

3 Insert the candleholders at a slight angle into a clay pot filled with plastic foam. Crush chocolate wafers, and layer them on top to create the "dirt."

Candy Stripes

Electrical tape adds a peppermint twist to a basic bud vase.

1 Wrap white electrical tape around a bud vase in an upward, diagonal pattern. Follow with red electrical tape to form a peppermint-striped effect.

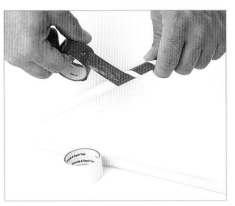

2 Cover a wooden dowel with white electrical tape, then with red electrical tape in the same manner as the vase. Repeat with a second dowel.

3 Secure the "peppermint stick" dowels together with a wired wood pick, then cover the wire with a matching piece of tape. Insert the pick into the vase.

This easy-to-assemble bud vase design features swirls of electrical tape wrapped to look like peppermint sticks. Nestled among sprigs of cedar, the white roses and clusters of snowberries *(Symphoricarpos)* incorporate the most traditional colors of the season, and the special candylike treatment gives the overall design a look that is both nostalgic and modern.

This affordable yet highly festive design is sure to convey a merry message to recipients, and the concept can be adapted to other elements as well. In addition to the bud vase and wooden dowels shown here, electrical tape can be used on other containers and props, offering a creative look for many styles of arrangements.

Ornamental Vases

A silvery glass ball makes a novel floral container.

The vessel is among the most noticed features of any floral design, and creations such as this one, which radiates from a Christmas ornament, are sure to draw attention. Simply remove the hanger from the top of the shimmering ball to create an opening for flowers.

With the help of a plastic flange, such as the center ring from a roll of ribbon or stem wrap, glued to the bottom of the ornament for stability, a charming mix of variegated pink-and-white miniature carnations and *Thryptomene calycina* is supported in the glassy orb. A slight tilt of the ornament enhances the design's visual appeal, which is accented by ruffles of wired ribbon with three miniature ornaments attached.

1 Select a large round plastic or glass ornament that is painted on the outside and has a large "opening." Remove the "crown" and hanger from the ornament.

2 Hot-glue a flange from a bolt of ribbon or, alternatively, the center from a roll of stem wrap to the bottom of the ornament.

3 Fill the ornament with flower food solution, and arrange floral materials. Tie wired ribbon around the "neck" of the ornament, and add millimeter balls.

Dramatic Dozen

Embrace an unexpected way to arrange 12 roses.

1 Arrange stems of baby's breath into a plastic trumpet vase to form a dense cluster just above the opening of the vase.

2 Attach two colored cable ties to each rose stem, just beneath the bloom. Curl the ties using the blunt side of a scissors blade in the same manner that you curl curling ribbon.

3 Arrange the roses through the baby's breath so that the blooms rest atop it. Rotate the curled cable ties to create a pleasing rhythm.

To create today's smart foliage-free aesthetic while still providing support for a gathering of stems, this arrangement includes the use of a lavish "field" of baby's breath. Surprisingly, it also incorporates colorful cable ties to bring rhythm to the dozen-rose delight.

The swirl of ties, zipped around the stems just beneath the blooms and curled with a scissors blade, mimics the color of the vase and brings this hip design together with its coordinating accessories.

Fun and flashy, this composition will attract both the young and the young-at-heart. Dozen-rose arrangements are popular gifts for nearly every occasion, and this novel approach will stand out among traditional roses designs.

Triple-Decker Roses

Showcase a dozen long-stemmed roses in an exciting new way.

This topiary-inspired dozen-rose arrangement is an exciting alternative to standard rose designs. The flowers are bundled and zip-tied in groups that increase in size as they descend from the topmost trio. Then, satiny pink bows, which pick up the blushing hue of the rose petals' reverse as well as the dusty pink color of the vase, are added to conceal the zip ties.

After the tiers are created and bound, the stems are all cut at once to a height that allows the final grouping of roses to rest upon the vase's lip. Wispy sprigs of tree fern are added as a collaring accent.

Despite its height, the arrangement is surprisingly stable. The container's tapered neck holds the dozen stems snugly and prevents tilting.

1 Gather three long-stemmed roses so the flower heads are even. Secure the bundle with a zip tie just below the rose heads.

2 About 6 inches down the trio's stems, gather four roses, and secure them with a zip tie. Repeat with the remaining five roses to create the final tier. Trim the zip-tie tails.

3 Tie bows below the top two levels to mask the zip ties. Cut all 12 rose stems to the same length, and drop the "topiary" into the vase.

1 Spray a clear glass vase with textured paint until the desired coverage is obtained.

2 Cut a length of sheer patterned ribbon, and double knot it around the base of the vase. Clip the tails at an angle.

3 Assemble a hand-tied bouquet, and cover the binding with ribbon. Cut the stems so their length allows the bouquet to rest just atop the vase.

Sweet Showpiece

Hand-tied roses drop into a customized glass vessel.

This fashionable hand-tied bouquet design is ideal for outfitting a casual wedding reception or other gathering and can be delivered for everyday celebrations as well.

Textured spray paint applied to the vessel enhances the pretty, complementary palette achieved by the 'Super Green' and 'Mi Amor!' roses. Meanwhile, the similarly colored ribbon treatment is simplified with just a casual knot and tails at the base rather than a traditional bow.

Reverse proportion characterizes this design since the container's height exceeds that of the bouquet it contains. A collar of trailing seeded *Eucalyptus* and the bow-adorned base avoid the appearance of a stark mound atop the narrow vase.

Fluted Roses

Fresh rose blossoms beautifully decorate toasting glasses.

The ceremonial toast, an important element of traditional weddings, anniversaries and other notable celebrations, is made more memorable with attractive, nontraditional toasting glass adornments.

Here, fresh rose blossoms elegantly enhance a pair of etched flutes for the bride and groom. The roses are separated from their calyxes and reflexed to envelop the glasses' stems. Floral adhesive is applied to the foot of each glass to hold the roses, as well as their foliage accents, in place.

While traditional enhancements remain popular, couples desiring something out of the ordinary will want to raise a glass to your creative talents.

1 Remove a rose bloom from its stem, grasping the petals so that the bloom remains intact.

2 Cup the bloom in the palm of your hand, and remove the center petals.

3 Apply floral adhesive to the base of a goblet. Separate the cluster of petals on one side, and position them around the stem of the goblet.

1 Form several stems of baby's breath into a simple hand-tied bouquet.

2 Place angel hair over the mound of baby's breath, gently pulling the angel hair to cover the tiny white blossoms.

3 Arrange roses into the framework created by the baby's breath and angel hair.

Holiday Dozen

Twelve roses are arranged with seasonal sparkle.

Resembling newly fallen snow, this festive design begins with a profusion of delicate white baby's breath *(Gypsophila)*. Atop the fluffy white mound, a thin layer of lustrous golden angel hair adds glimmer and contributes to the sturdiness of the baby's-breath armature, through which the materials are arranged.

Once it is formed, gorgeous scarlet-hued 'Freedom' and snowy white 'Escimo' roses are inserted into the angel-hair-and-baby's-breath structure. To achieve the yuletide pizzazz, pine cones and sprigs of Douglas fir *(Pseudotsuga)* are tucked into the rosy gathering. The frosted glass vase adds to the design's captivating snowy appeal.

Customized Carafes

Gorgeous garden roses gleam inside vintage-looking vessels.

Informal milk-jug-shaped vases, adorned with hand-cut bands of green and gold mesh fabric, are elevated to the status of trendy vessels for exhibiting glamorized garden roses under glass. The fabulous and fragrant varieties featured here include 'Toulouse-Lautrec,' 'Quatre-Coeurs' and 'Antique Romantica.'

In addition to the glitzy banding, the mesh fabric also embellishes a few tucked-in *Galax* leaves, which nestle among the differently sized blossoms and repeat the sparkly splendor.

Create these special gifts in multiples for eye-catching tabletop displays at special events or throughout the home. For full-bloomed garden roses in a bolder color palette, choose varieties in burgundy, deep red and hot pink.

1 Spray adhesive onto several *Galax* leaves. Press a small section of mesh fabric onto each leaf, and trim to the shape of each leaf.

2 Fold mesh fabric into a multilayer gathering, and trim a narrow band from one end.

3 Spray adhesive onto the neck of the milk-jug vase, and wrap the mesh strip around the vase. Secure with additional spray adhesive.

1 Place a round crocheted doily over the opening of a ginger-jar-shaped container or any container with a "neck."

2 Tie the doily around the neck of the container with a thin ribbon, raffia or other material of your choice.

3 Cut out the center of the doily over the opening of the vase, fill the vase with flower-food solution and arrange flowers.

Rose Bowl

A dainty doily collar feminizes a rose and carnation collection.

This classic round mass of creamy white roses is exceedingly feminine and traditional, despite the lack of the often indispensible and obligatory baby's breath and other filler flowers. Rather than those typically beloved ingredients, this elegant arrangement features an updated and somewhat unexpected technique — blush pink carnations placed deep within the design, forming a fresh framework of stems into which the roses are arranged.

The carnations provide a lovely soft color contrast and luxurious depth. And the premium foliage, arranged prominently in the design, takes on a more important role than just background filler material. A creamy crocheted doily contributes a touch of romance to the composition.

Framed Flowers

Lushly gathered roses are surrounded by tufts of baby's breath.

For a new take on the classic "roses in a vase" design, appropriate for any gift-giving occasion, try this modern composition. It resembles a plane of apricot-hued roses arranged pavé style amid an ethereal cloud of 'Million Stars' *Gypsophila* (baby's breath).

A sleek tapered vase in a modern square shape adds an interesting look to the design, but the geometric opening offers a functional purpose as well; it's shaped just right to hold a decorative grid into which the florals are arranged. The structure is easily assembled using bamboo and raffia and is nestled into the vase. The vase's tapered walls ensure that the grid remains snugly in place.

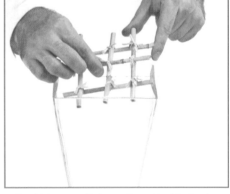

1 Make a small decorative grid with six pieces of bamboo and raffia that will fit snugly into the top of a square glass vase.

2 Arrange stems of baby's breath in the vase, around the perimeter, to create a fluffy border for the roses.

3 Arrange a dozen short-stemmed roses in the center of the vase on the same level as the baby's breath for a contemporary styling.

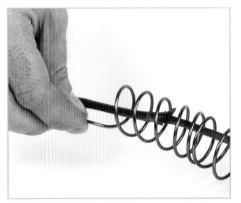

1 To create coiled "springs", wrap a length of wire around a tube. Slide the coiled wire onto a rose stem, and wrap the wire tightly at the bottom of the stem to hold it in place.

2 To create decorative spirals, carefully roll long pieces of wire into spirals with a pair of needle-nose pliers, then bend the ends down to form picks.

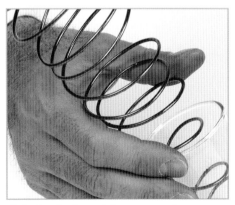

3 For the "tornado" armature, twist an extra-long piece of wire into a cone shape, and place the armature into a clear bud vase.

Wired Roses

Playful additions add a twist to a traditional rose arrangement.

Rather than serving a functional purpose, as the wiring of roses once did to support stems and prevent bent neck, these inventive wiring techniques are primarily decorative. Here, two variations form fun and useful shapes for arranging fresh florals into bud vases.

In the vase on the left, roses and *Pittosporum* are arranged through a coiled wire armature that holds the flowers upright and reduces the amount of flowers and foliage needed to fill the vase. Handcrafted spiral picks are added with the *Pittosporum* to complete the design.

In the vase on the right, roses are arranged through "springs" made of the same wire. Again, the wires help fill the vase and are echoed by the added picks.

Burning Desires

Hot candy vases convey passionate sentiments.

Try this fun twist for a red-hot yet affordable bud-vase option. The younger set especially will love these spicy gifts.

Inside cellophane bags that feature clear windows at their midsections, fiery cinnamon imperials candies anchor clear vases. Tightly tying the bags at the vases' necks ensures that the candies stay dry and ready to consume when the floral show is over.

Given the value-added presentation that belies the low price of these delectable gifts, it's a bit of a surprise that no long stems are needed here. Instead, the roses are nestled into cooling clouds of baby's breath. A double-sided red-and-white ribbon in contemporary geometric patterns ties the color scheme together in a playful finishing touch.

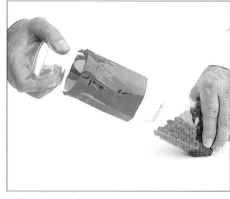

1 Fill a cellophane bag about one-quarter full with cinnamon imperials candies. Slip a clear bud vase into the bag, and fill the vase with flower-food solution.

2 Cinch the cellophane bag's opening around the neck of the bud vase. Encircle it with a length of transparent tape to keep it cinched.

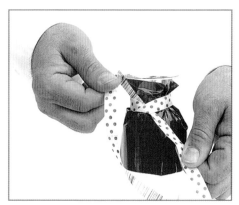

3 Cut a length of ribbon approximately three times the height of the vase. Tie it around the neck of the vase, and lightly curl the ribbon ends with a scissors edge.

Potted Roses

Freeze-dried roses look fresh but offer long-lasting home display.

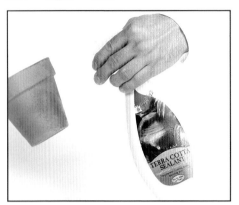

Matching the vibrant hues of these ultra-fresh-looking freeze-dried roses, a trio of clay pots is easily customized with bold decorator colors. A terra-cotta sealant prevents the porous clay from absorbing the paint, so less is required, making the process fast and affordable.

Once the paint is dry, create these enchanting decoratives by first filling the pots with Spanish moss. Then, simply hot-glue the freeze-dried flowers atop the mossy filling. Preserved bear grass, cut into bits and tucked into the gaps between the blooms, increases dimension and contributes a modern flair. These simple yet striking designs are wonderful for use in multiples—throughout a single room or an entire home or workplace.

1 Spray the exterior and inside rim of a clay pot with a terra-cotta sealant. This will reduce the amount of paint needed to cover the pot.

2 Apply two or three light coats of spray paint in a color that coordinates with the chosen florals. When the paint has dried, fill the pot with Spanish moss.

3 Hot-glue freeze-dried roses atop the moss. Cut preserved bear grass into 3-inch-long strips, and arrange small bunches of the grass between the blooms.

Verdant Sheaf

Fresh flowers lavishly encircle a gathering of grains and branches.

Formed into a sheaf that appears gathered by hand under the golden rays of an autumn sun, a bundle of foxtail millet *(Setaria)* pairs with birch twigs in this exquisite presentation. While the twigs lend a woody texture to the ripened grains, they also bring the urn's earthy hue into the arrangement, creating a unified look between the florals and their container.

At the sheaf's base, a breathtaking mix of gardeny green materials, including 'Limona' roses, 'Kermit' spray mums, 'Lady Green' carnations and *Hydrangeas*, is accented with seeded *Eucalyptus*, which echoes the woody feel imparted by the birch branches and also helps continue the color transition from earthy brown to organic green.

1 Grasp several stems of foxtail millet *(Setaria)*, and arrange the small bundles vertically, one at a time, into the center of a block of saturated floral foam to create a "sheaf."

2 Arrange several birch branchlets at a slight angle around the millet sheaf so that the birch flares out slightly.

3 Arrange fresh flowers in the floral-foam-filled urn, around the base of the sheaf.

1 Wire one bunch of rye at a 45-degree angle to the handle, where it attaches to the basket.

2 Wire another bunch of rye in the opposite direction of the first, forming an "X" with the two bunches.

3 Attach a third bunch of rye with the heads pointing downward. Fan the three bunches out. Repeat these steps on the opposite side of the basket.

Bountiful Exotics

Classics pair with the unexpected in this harvest basket.

With matching groups of dried rye fastened to its handles, this basket appears to overflow with harvested grains; however, the diminutive rye sheaves are created with just three tiny bunches.

Inside the basket, rich textures and harvest hues take center stage, despite that the combination of materials used is not entirely traditional. For example, exotic materials, such as the sundrenched *Vanda* orchids and deep-purple fern curls, stand out among the other seasonal favorites — burgundy artichokes, brown sunflower centers and golden billy buttons *(Craspedia)* and cockscomb *(Celosia)*.

A perfect combination of traditional favorites and unusual additions, this creation is sure to be an attention getter.

Beribboned Sheaf

A goldenrod sheaf rises from within a circle of radiant florals.

Forming the top tier of this mono-chromatic two-tier design, a generous plume of goldenrod *(Solidago)* erupts from the center of a wreathlike ring of exquisite blossoms. These materials—roses, lilies and button spray mums—harmoniously compose the lower tier and surround the fluffy fountain in golden grandeur.

Between the two tiers, streamers of ribbon, selected to match the teal-painted clay pot, are tied to each of the goldenrod insertions like tiny teal flags. The flags, in gorgeous bold contrast to the luminous flaxen hues, highlight the separate areas and encourage visual flow from top to bottom. Due to the design's multitiered visual complexity, a soothing mono-chromatic floral palette is ideal.

1 Squeeze some acrylic craft paint onto a clay pot. Spread it around with your fingers, completely covering the pot. Line the pot with foil, and add floral foam.

2 Arrange stems of *Solidago* into the center of the pot. Tie a 6-inch piece of wire-edge ribbon to each stem of *Solidago* just below the blooms.

3 Arrange flowers and foliage around the edge of the pot. Pull out the ends of the ribbon, and shape into curves over the flowers.

Harvest Gathering

Ripened fall fruits spill from within a grain-covered basket.

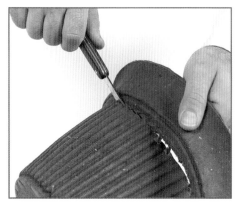

1 Carefully cut off the flared rim of a papier-mâché pot with a sharp knife.

2 Hot-glue barley between the pot's ridges, alternating grain head placement, pointing one up and the next down. Cover the pot, reserving cut stems.

3 Apply a second layer of barley and reserved stems in the same alternating fashion. Secure with waterproof tape. Conceal the tape with wrappings of jute.

Covered with a sheaf of dried barley and filled with sectioned clusters of fresh flowers and artichokes—a technique that showcases the vegetative types and emphasizes their compelling textures—a papier-mâché pot resembles a decorated bushel basket overflowing with fall's abundant harvest. The lush composition achieves its soothing palette with a multitude of floral materials in greens, browns and golds—billy buttons *(Craspedia)*, *Scabiosa* pods, cockscomb *(Celosia)*, sneezeweed *(Helenium)*, cone flowers *(Echinacea)* and China millet.

Since most papier-mâché vessels are coated with a substance to make them watertight, no liner is typically required. Verify that yours is watertight before filling with saturated floral foam.

Symbol of Prosperity

Dried grains are formed into a show-stopping sheaf.

Symbolic of bounteous harvests, sheaflike designs are quintessential autumn decoratives. This distinctive example, ideal as a centerpiece, mantel decoration or any type of table accessory, has a plastic foam cone as its core and is composed of three types of dried grains: bearded wheat *(Triticum)*, rye *(Secale)* and reed grass *(Phalaris)*.

To add a splash of color, especially for impact when matching a particular décor, replace one of these honey-hued materials with something that is naturally colorful, or opt for a dyed version. In either case, you also could replace the straw-colored raffia with a binding material to match the more vividly hued grains, which will carry the color story to the shocklike, stem-covered cone.

1 Bind several bunches of grains just under the heads. Cut 3 or 4 inches off the bottom portion of a 15-inch-tall plastic-foam cone, and insert the top portion into the center of the bundle.

2 Bind the grain stems to the cone with raffia, then cut off the heads. Invert the cut-off bottom of the cone, and secure it into the top of the "shock" with low-temp glue.

3 Make small bundles of the various grain heads by binding two or three stems with steel picks. Arrange bundles into the inverted bottom of the cone to form a dense mound.

1 Fill a vessel with dry or plastic foam, and conceal the foam with sheet moss. Arrange foxgloves into the foam, and arrange birch branches around the foxglove stems.

2 Use pliable vine or bark-covered wire to fasten together a square armature. Place the armature around the branch-and-foxglove bundle, and secure it in place with wire.

3 Clip the berry stems short, and wire the berry bunches to the square armature, forming a berried collar around the foxglove stems.

Sculpted Plume

Permanent berries encircle a fountain of fabric foxgloves.

This tiered composition, which is much taller than it is wide to emphasize a modern ambience, makes a dramatic statement in contemporary settings. It is recommended for almost year-round display—in pairs for buffets, credenzas and other long tabletops, or singly for placement anywhere a strong vertical presence is desired.

Other tall, sculptural materials may replace the foxgloves, as needed, for dimension or color. Consider vibrant *Delphiniums*, with their delicate blue blossoms, or voluminous snapdragons and stocks, which are available in a range of botanically correct colors. Select berries and containers to match or complement the floral sheaves.

Stick To It

Cinnamon sticks cover a container filled with stunning botanicals.

Textural layers of aromatic stick cinnamon, easily applied to a ribbed papier-mâché pot with hot-melt (pan) glue, tastefully enhance an abundance of flowers and fruit.

The spice's tawny hue and rustic vertical lines result in a dramatic base for the glorious collection of miniature callas, persimmons, and cockscomb, the latter of which is arranged into the foam around the pot's perimeter like a ruffly velvet collar. The remaining materials, including budding branches of red *Hibiscus* that extend the impressive design's spatial value, are arranged within the cockscomb boundary.

This gorgeous arrangement will be at home in just about any location since its enticing natural palette complements many modern decór schemes.

1 Remove the flared rim of a papier-mâché pot. Cut the tops of the cinnamon sticks to an even height, just above the top of the pot. Reserve the cut pieces.

2 Apply hot-melt (pan) glue between the ridges of the pot's exterior, and press cinnamon sticks into the glue, with the bottoms of the sticks flush with the bottom of the pot.

3 Using more hot-melt glue, affix the reserved pieces of cut cinnamon sticks atop the first layer of sticks to form a multidimensional, beltlike layer.

1 Affix dried rose petals to a plastic-wrapped foam ball with spray adhesive.

2 Wrap permanent twig vine over the orb to create a "cage." Secure vine ends into the foam with steel picks.

3 Hot-glue butterflies in random fashion around the vine "cage."

Butterflies and Blooms

Permanent twig vines encircle a petal-covered sphere.

Several types of butterflies alight on a structure of permanent vines in this pretty arrangement, which would be a fun highlight to a young girl's room.

The vining cage surrounds a foam orb that is covered with dried rose petals in pretty pinks and lemony yellows. Adding to the organic quality of the display is the weathered, moss-covered pot, which suggests that this composition was rescued from the elements, bringing along with it the group of fluttering friends.

Instead of butterflies, other charming insects could be used, if desired, especially dragonflies, bumblebees and lady bugs — whatever the recipients' favored creatures might be.

Sunflower Field

Willow branches impart a "wild" feel to cultivated sunflowers.

A chic, golden-glass vessel, the oval perimeter of which is lined with a vegetative hedge of pussy-willow branches and bear grass, imparts this simple collection of sunflowers with modern presence. The brilliant blossoms, which are available year-round, are arranged in a gentle flowing manner, culminating in a pair of *Galax* leaf accents.

Dynamic curly-willow branches and additional blades of bear grass inserted among the sunny blooms contribute an untended, garden-grown quality, enhancing the organic appeal.

Use this design at any time of the year as a gift or to accessorize a space. Replace the sunflowers as needed.

1 Fill the vase with saturated floral foam. Insert pussy-willow branches around the perimeter of the vase, leaving the center open. Trim the branches to a uniform height.

2 Add several blades of bear grass to the pussy-willow hedge. Tuck mosses between the pussy-willow branches to fill open spaces.

3 Arrange sunflowers into the floral foam. Add curly willow and bear grass randomly among the sunflowers. Accessorize with *Galax* leaves.

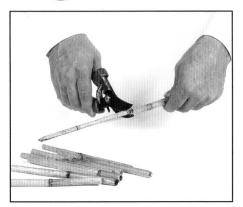

1 Cut pieces of bamboo 1 inch longer that the height of the pot. Line up the pieces with all wide ends together and all narrow ends together. A natural fan shape will form.

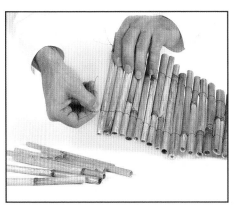

2 Wire the bamboo together, one piece at a time, using four pieces of paddle wire, two near the top and two near the bottom. Twist the wires once around each stem.

3 Place the fencelike structure around the pot, with the narrow ends on the bottom and the wide ends on top. Wire the ends of the "fence" together.

Bamboozle Cover-up

Customize a pretty plant with a botanical pot cover.

Plants, like this long-lasting azalea *(Rhododendron)*, in a fiery pink hue, are popular year-round for gift-giving and home display. But for maximum eye appeal, basic growers' pots can be concealed with attractive enhancements.

This custom-crafted covering, lending a tropical- or Asian-inspired flair, is an ideal option. The botanical pot wrapper is created by wiring together equal-length pieces of river cane, or bamboo. Once finished, the pot cover can be secured to the pot with wire or glue, or it simply can be placed around a pot and set in a saucer, making it reusable for other plants.

Just about any type of plant material would dazzle inside this container treatment. But with its hint of Asian influence, the bamboo covering is perfect for orchids and other exotics.

Tabletop Forest

Flowers and feathers nestle inside a branchy thicket.

Among a "forest" of vertically arranged birch branches, all trimmed to the same height, vibrant yellow and yellowish green florals are placed. Exhibiting a diversity of size, shape and texture, the materials range from sleek callas to textural pods and exotic kangaroo paws *(Anigozanthos)*.

While some items, such as the montbretia *(Crocosmia)* pods and the turkey feathers, are arranged low and among the branches, most of the blossoms are positioned just above the tops of the branches, creating a flowering "hedge" effect—a distinctive centerpiece form.

Pea gravel, placed atop the floral foam, creates the forest's "ground cover" and repeats the natural colors and textures of the rough-hewn planter.

1 Fill a rectangular planter with saturated floral foam. Cover the foam with pea gravel.

2 Cut birch branches into 8-inch pieces, and arrange them into the floral foam in a hedgelike manner.

3 Arrange assorted flowers and feathers among the branches, with the blooms positioned just above the branches.

Hot and Hip

Fresh-cut carnation stems provide a bed for peppery pieces.

1 Cover a floral-foam sphere with carnation blooms, the stems of which are each trimmed to the same length.

2 Strip the leftover carnation stems of all their foliage.

3 Cut the carnation stems into varying lengths, and fill the bowls with them. Place peppers and carnation-covered orbs inside the bowls.

A contemporary table alternative, usable whenever the bell-shaped vegetables are in season, this design features orange peppers and apricot-hued standard carnations. Some of the crisp peppers are placed into orange tumblers while others are added to a bowl containing carnation stems and saturated floral-foam spheres covered with fresh carnation blooms.

When appropriate, the crisp peppers can be used in place of the round orange fruit of another plant—the pumpkin—making these stemmed creations applicable to multiple holidays, events and seasons. In addition, other varieties of bell peppers, with delectable red, yellow and green skins, also could pair with similarly hued carnations.

Flowering Bonsai

Permanent *Magnolia* branches are shaped into a treelike form.

With the Asian influence strong in American home décor, bonsai, which originated in China more than 1,000 years ago, is as popular as ever in the United States.

Here, the trendy look of bonsai is re-created with a single permanent *Magnolia* stem. The pliable wired branches are manipulated in every direction to create a rhythmic growth pattern of buds and blossoms. The "trunk" is inserted into a plastic-foam sphere, which is then covered with moss. The aged finish of the pot is a perfect complement.

Experiment with shaping the stems into several configurations. Just as no two bonsai trees are alike, customers will appreciate a selection of this distinctive permanent *Magnolia* style as well.

1 Bore a hole through a plastic-foam sphere, and insert a permanent *Magnolia* branch through the sphere. Shape the base of the branch into a spiral formation.

2 Mix plaster solution, and pour it into the pot, filling the pot about half full. Set the foam sphere into the pot, with the spiraled base of the branch in the plaster solution.

3 Cover the exposed portion of the foam sphere with moss, securing the moss to the sphere with greening pins.

1 Fill a pot with plastic foam, and lay a twig wreath atop the pot. Dip hyacinth stakes into hot-melt (pan) glue, and insert the stakes through the wreath and into the foam.

2 Insert wood picks or hyacinth stakes into permanent pears. Dip the ends of the picks or stakes into glue, and insert them into the foam within the center of the wreath.

3 Arrange florals in a circular pattern around the wreath, tucking the tulips' leaves in to continue the circular motion. Swirl vines and branches atop and around the wreath.

Windswept Wreath

Permanent florals grace a wreath-topped container.

Arranged around the perimeter of a twig wreath with an inherently wild quality, swirled permanent vines and foliated branches, accompanied by graceful fabric parrot tulips and soft berry sprays, compose a tabletop decorative of captivating untamed beauty.

For visual weight amid the dynamic circular motion, a cluster of luscious permanent pears is nestled within the wreath's center, peeking coyly from inside the swirling shroud of permanent botanicals.

Depending on the décor of the space, this arrangement can be displayed in a home or office throughout the year. And since it is secured atop a weathered clay vessel with long hyacinth stakes, the wreath is stable, even in high-traffic environments.

Luscious Orb

Preserved *Hydrangea* florets compose a realistic topiary form.

Several branches of curly willow, used to create a naturalistic "trunk," support a floral-foam orb covered with preserved *Hydrangeas* to create this striking topiary. Three hues of the preserved blossoms, all in the same color family, create depth and visual intrigue on the elevated sphere.

The curly-willow branches are inserted into dry-floral foam, which is covered with potting soil to replicate fresh earth. A few individual *Hydrangea* petals placed atop the soil look as if a breeze blew them to the ground.

This arrangement would be lovely on a mantel or sideboard—anywhere height is needed. And since the curly willow will dry in place, this topiary can decorate a space for extended periods.

1 Insert curly-willow branches into dry-floral foam to form a "trunk." Spray the foam with adhesive, and spread potting soil over the top, shaking off any excess. Repeat layering.

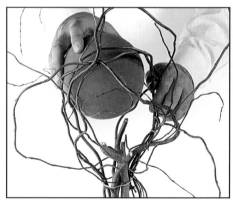

2 Impale a floral-foam sphere onto the curly-willow "trunk," and arrange the willow tendrils, which are secured just below, around the sphere.

3 Tape the stems of the *Hydrangeas* into bunches using stem wrap, and arrange the bunches into the floral-foam sphere.

Topiary Twist

A new and all-natural look for a traditional topiary-style design.

1 Bind several amaryllises together with stem wrap. Insert them into a floral-foam-filled pot.

2 Wrap a fresh leaf around the stem wrap, and secure it with liquid adhesive.

3 Place pussy willows, cut to 3- and 4-inch lengths and bundled with aluminum wire, on top of the pot. Insert hairpin wires into the foam to hold the bundles in place.

Instead of wearing a ribbon adornment like many traditional topiaries, the "necks" of these beautiful amaryllises *(Hippeastrums)* are decoratively wrapped with a polypody fern leaf. The bundle of blossoms stands tall inside the floral-foam-filled pot, bound just beneath the blooms with stem wrap. The leaf, which camouflages the stem wrap and is adhered with a dab of liquid adhesive, adds visual support to the lengthy stems.

The all-natural look the leaf creates is continued in the bird's-nestlike appearance at the "plant's" base. Bundled pussy willows rest atop a mossy base and mirror the pointed, somewhat wild appearance of the amaryllis blooms. Similarly, the pot mirrors the smooth, sleek appearance of the amaryllis stems.

Soft and Sweet

Faded pinks highlight an interpretive topiary of lilies.

Monobotanical arrangements are classic favorites that offer plenty of opportunities for creative styling as is demonstrated with this topiary-inspired arrangement of fragrant Oriental lilies and *Equisetum*.

The blush-pink colorations in the breathtaking blossoms, combined with the faded stenciling on the containers (a beautiful complement to the flowers), achieve a feminine aesthetic. Women of similar sensibilities will appreciate its sweet sentiments for a host of occasions.

In addition, the pretty vessel becomes a cherished remembrance of the sender's sentiments since it can be used to hold everything from plants to pencils after the elegant lilies fade.

1 Cut a column of saturated floral foam slightly smaller than the interior of the container. Place the foam vertically in the container, leaving space between it and the inside of the vessel.

2 Place pieces of *Equisetum* vertically around the column of foam. Trim the top ends of the *Equisetum* even, as tall as you want the "trunk" to be.

3 Arrange lilies into the foam, making sure to insert the stems all the way through the foam to the bottom of the container.

1 Fill a container with floral foam. Place a glass cylinder vase atop the foam. Insert branches or woody stems around the vase to create a "trunk" and to hold the cylinder in place.

2 Wrap a heavy-gauge wire with brown stem wrap, and tightly bind it around the branches near the top of the cylinder.

3 Remove all foliage from the tulips. Fill the cylinder vase with bulb-flower-food solution, and arrange the tulips in the vase. Add *Galax* leaves around the rim of the vase.

Woodsy "Tulipary"

Branches conceal a traditional vase arrangement.

Because tulips in mass best lend themselves to arrangement in vases, a glass cylinder elevated atop a pot filled with floral foam is an ideal system for designing a natural-looking tulip topiary. The glass receptacle is surrounded by woody stems, disguising the fact that these fabulous blossoms are simply composed in a traditional manner. In addition, the flowers' rare ability to elongate and stretch is not at all impended.

Composing this dramatic design, which has a multitude of applications, 'La Courtine' French tulips are paired with smaller bicolor tulips. The flowers are stripped of their foliage, and rounded *Galax* leaves become striking stand-ins.

Topiary Nest

Unusual ingredients expand the boundaries of a traditional design.

Created in a traditional manner and shape, this inventive topiary is chock-full of uncommon components, making it perfect for customers who are looking for something thought provoking, out of the ordinary or especially creative to spice up a home or business interior.

Achieving those objectives, one bunch of foxtail millet *(Setaria)* is tied with raffia and inserted into dry-floral foam, which is covered with preserved *Galax* leaves and a variety of mosses and lichens. This creates the look of a forest floor, and the weathered clay pot also complements this "natural" look. The addition of a bird's nest, complete with a pair of wooden eggs, puts a welcome but unexpected twist on the composition.

1 Tie one bunch of *Setaria* with raffia, and insert the bundle into dry-floral foam.

2 Glue a bird's nest to a wood pick, and insert the pick into the middle of the *Setaria* bundle.

3 Cover the foam with leaves, mosses and lichens to create the effect of a forest floor.

1 Fold a sheet of craft foam in half, and cut the foam into the desired purse shape.

2 Staple the sides to form a pocket. Remove the stems from *Galax* leaves, spray the backsides with adhesive and layer them onto the pocket in an overlapping manner, beginning at the top.

3 Punch holes into the corners of the open end of the pouch. Thread two lengths of 1/4-inch-wide ribbon through the holes, and tie them to form "straps."

Botanical Clutch

A handmade pouch serves as a flower-filled handbag.

Rather than risking damage to real purses, create your own pocketbooks that can fashionably hold all types of blossoms.

Here, inexpensive craft foam is formed into a small pouch and covered with overlapping *Galax* leaves. The tiny tote is filled with a wealth of Guernsey lilies *(Nerines)* in water tubes that are hot-glued inside the custom-crafted bag. Serving as handles, narrow striped ribbon streamers finish the creation and enable the *Nerine*-filled bag to be securely carried at proms, weddings and other special events.

To avoid pollen stains, be sure to remove the anthers from all pollen-bearing blossoms. Or, alternatively, select those without pollen. Just about any type of bloom can be used, including big blossoms; simply create a larger pouch.

Glitzy Tote

A flowery pocketbook replaces a traditional corsage or bouquet.

This intensely fuchsia tote bag is a fanciful repository for a collection of radiant 'Everglades' spray chrysanthemums, which are placed into water picks so they remain hydrated and vibrant. Adhered to the sides of the tote, several "fans" of *Ruscus* leaves extend the flowers' visual presence. And to add glamour, tiny, sparkling jewel-encrusted bows adorn the bases of the handles.

The energetic complementary color combination lends itself to use by the younger set, especially for proms. But with the faceted bow additions, this flowery satchel also could be used in place of a traditional bouquet for a wedding ceremony and perhaps even as a corsage replacement for a mother-of-the-bride who is young at heart.

1 Apply several *Ruscus* leaves to the sides of the tote in fan-shaped patterns using spray adhesive. Glue a piece of plastic foam into the tote's base.

2 Place several stems of spray mums into water picks, and glue the picks into the plastic foam inside the bag.

3 Pin jeweled bows to the handles of the purse, one at each of the four points where the straps meet the bag.

Petaled Perfection

An updated version of a traditional flower-girl basket.

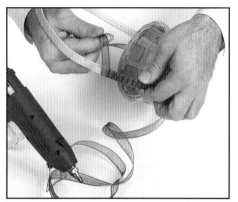

1 Wrap the basket's handle with narrow ribbon, securing it in place occasionally with tiny dabs of hot glue. If you choose a sheer ribbon, overlap it slightly to create a striped effect.

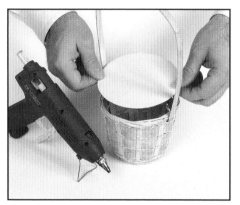

2 Cut a circular piece of cardboard the same diameter as the opening of the basket, and secure it to the basket with hot glue.

3 Using liquid adhesive, cover the basket and its cardboard top with individual stock florets. Adorn the bases of the handles with bows and spray roses.

Flower girls have forever carried petal-filled baskets down the aisles at wedding ceremonies, dropping the petals as they go to make pretty paths for the brides. But this practice often comes with a messy cleanup, with flower fragments ground into carpets and stains created on aisle runners. So a flower-covered basket, in a departure from tradition, provides a perfect solution.

Individual florets of sweetly scented stocks *(Matthiola)* are glued onto the basket using liquid adhesive as well as onto the cardboard disc that covers its opening, which creates the illusion that the basket is filled with the flowers. A flourish of spray roses is glued to each end of the handle, adhered to bows made from the same ribbon that elegantly enwraps the handle.

Grand Rose Satchel

A leaf-covered "basket" replaces traditional options for flower girls.

Covered with a layer of *Galax* leaves and filled with what resembles a large composite rose, this diminutive "satchel" makes a fabulous nature-inspired alternative for all types of formal and semiformal occasions. The "bag," however, is actually formed from plastic foam, and the pair of organic-looking handles are made from bark-covered wire that has been braided.

For the lavish rose presentation, individual petals are glued around the perimeter of the plastic foam, and a single exquisite 'Eliza' rose blossom is placed in a water pick that is glued into the center.

This rosy presentation can be accessorized, as needed, with a simple tie of ribbon or a few modest jewels.

1 Cut off the bottom of a plastic-foam cone to create a tapered, 3- to 4-inch-high piece, or carve a block to shape. Spray *Galax* leaves with adhesive, and apply them to the plastic foam.

2 Braid lengths of bark-covered wire to form two straplike handles. Press the ends of the handles into the plastic foam, and secure with hot glue.

3 Place a single rose into a water pick, and insert the pick into the center of the plastic foam. Glue rose petals around the perimeter of the plastic foam with floral adhesive. Fill gaps with additional petals.

1 Carve a small sphere of floral foam, insert a short chenille stem and tie the ends together to form a loop from which the sphere can hang. Wrap the sphere with fine-gauge wire.

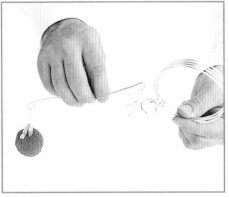

2 Coil wire into a bracelet. Wrap more wire tightly around the bracelet, and form a dangling loop. Shape another wire into an S-hook; secure one end to the bracelet and the other to the sphere.

3 Scrunch two long strands of bullion wire into small balls. Flatten the balls, and attach them with floral adhesive to the design, obscuring the points where the pieces are hooked together.

Pomander Corsage

Craft a dramatic wrist accent for a wedding or sweetheart dance.

This ingenious pomander corsage is the perfect accompaniment for older flower girls, junior bridesmaids or other wedding party members. It's also a sensational showcase for teens headed to a sweetheart dance or prom.

Although it might appear to be fragile, its deceptively simple construction is remarkably secure, to withstand the rigors of celebratory events. The blossoms in the pomander are secured into a floral-foam sphere with stem adhesive.

Silver-hued foliages mirror the sparkle from the jeweled picks and loosely draped bullion wire. The wire also is used to form jewel-like embellishments that accent the bracelet and help hide the mechanics.

Floral Choker

This botanical necklace offers a flowery twist on wedding jewelry.

Floral jewelry is a fabulous trend in both wedding and prom flowers. And with the variety of decorative wires on the market, it is easier than ever to be creative with fashion accessories. That's evident in this design, which utilizes a combination of wires, both aluminum and bullion, to create a fun and flirty custom piece of jewelry for modern-minded women.

Miniature *Cymbidiums* impart a tropical look, which is complemented by the vibrant orange 'Mambo' spray roses and *Gerbera*, from which some of the petals are removed. These are glued in a layered fashion to the cascading loop of wire.

The trendy choker complements a variety of necklines and a variety of fashion colors as well.

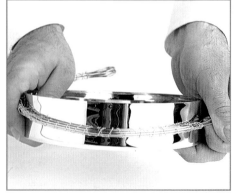

1 Create a choker by looping aluminum wire back and forth until a desired thickness is achieved. Coil bullion wire around the choker, then shape it around a circular container.

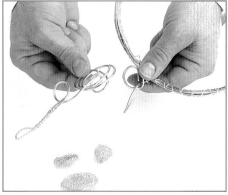

2 Shape a length of aluminum wire into an abstract "pendant," and wire it to the necklace. Roll bullion wire into balls, press them into medallions, and wire them to the pendant.

3 Remove a few petals from a *Gerbera*, and adhere all flowers, petals and foliage to the necklace and pendant with floral adhesive.

1 Make a multiloop bow with No. 3- or No. 5-width double-face satin ribbon. Tie the bow in the center with the same ribbon, long enough for the wearer to tie around her wrist.

2 Glue roses and feathers among the ribbon loops using liquid adhesive. Set aside until the adhesive dries.

3 Cut gold-colored pearl-head corsage pins in half. Dip the shortened pins into liquid adhesive, and insert them into the centers of the roses — one, three or five per blossom.

Wrist Options

A not-so-standard corsage for proms and weddings.

Coveted by many teenage girls, roses are standards for prom corsages. But that doesn't mean that all such corsages have to look similar or be void of personality, which is critical since no fashionable teen wants to don the same corsage that everyone else is wearing.

This sophisticated monochromatic composition, created with diminutive 'Jana' spray roses, champagne-colored pearl accents, luxurious double-face satin ribbon and a few fluffy feathers, is a classic example. And the custom touches are quick to add. The materials are simply glued into a multiloop bow, and the pearly pins are inserted into the blooms.

In addition to proms, this shimmering corsage could be worn at wedding ceremonies as well.

Verdant Posy

A monochromatic bouquet for modern brides and maids.

Green has emerged as a popular color for contemporary weddings, giving a natural, botanical feeling to settings from gardeny to glamorous.

This bouquet, at a glance, makes it difficult to distinguish the flowers from the foliages. All are arranged among one another, with a "rose" created from Algerian ivy *(Hedera canariensis)* as the focal point. Variegated *Aspidistra* leaves and oregonia add creamy highlights, and young Queen Anne's lace *(Ammi)* adds texture with its fluffy white tips. Swirls of lily grass *(Liriope)* lend motion.

The materials are arranged into a straight-handle bouquet holder, which is secured inside a decorative cover. The cover continues the monochrome palette and completes a stylishly tailored appearance.

1 Roll an ivy leaf in half vertically, then in half again. Repeat this step with a second leaf.

2 Put the rolled leaves together, and pierce a wire through the bottom.

3 Add flat leaves around the rolled leaves, and secure the stems with floral tape.

1 Cluster three to five *Muscaris*, and wrap their stems with stem wrap. Cut the stems at an angle with a sharp knife or snips for easier insertion into the bouquet holder.

2 Insert small wood picks into the hyacinth stems. Glue the wood picks into the bouquet holder with floral adhesive.

3 Secure discarded stems around the bouquet holder handle with waterproof tape, then glue a tulip leaf around the tape.

Stem Covering

Achieve a hand-tied look with the water source of a holder.

This spectacular composition maintains the appearance of a hand-tied bouquet; however, it is designed in a bouquet holder. Stems are taped around the handle to conceal it, and the tape is cleverly disguised with a fresh tulip leaf.

In addition to its organic appeal, this bouquet features a striking combination of colors. The tulips, stars-of-Bethlehem *(Ornithogalums)*, amaryllises, yellow hyacinths and glory lilies *(Gloriosas)* add warm hues to the design while the lavender hyacinths and diminutive grape hyacinths *(Muscaris)* contribute cool colors.

This stemmed handle treatment can be utilized any time a bride wants a hand-tied look but the flowers require a water source.

Sparkling Composite

Bring on the bling with a jeweled heirloom addition.

1 Hot-glue a ribbon flange onto a cone-shaped bouquet holder.

The elaborate rhinestone pin centered in this rosette of 'Toscana' *Alstroemeria* petals illustrates how a family heirloom can be incorporated beautifully and creatively into a bridal bouquet. The piece of jewelry, in addition to being sentimentally significant, adds dramatic flair to the otherwise simple arrangement.

A collar of rose leaves positioned beneath the petals adds texture and dimension to the bouquet, and the holder creates unity within the arrangement by emphasizing the dark pink accents on the *Alstroemeria* petals.

Despite its glamorous appearance, this bouquet is simple and inexpensive to create. And, in addition to being a great value, it is sure to increase the emotional value of the bride's special day.

2 Make a collar by gluing rose leaves to the flange's underside with floral adhesive. Glue the flower petals onto the top side of the flange, working from the outside in.

3 Hot-glue a pin or other jewelry onto a wood pick. Dispense hot glue around the bottom portion of the pick, and insert the pick into the bouquet holder.

Posy for a Princess

Elegant accents decorate a cluster of casual blooms.

1 Make several bows, each with six to 10 loops, from ribbons of various colors and widths. Attach each bow to a small wired wood pick, and insert into a decorative bouquet cover.

2 Cut several daisy spray mums to 1-inch-long (or longer) stem lengths. Apply liquid adhesive to each stem, and arrange the flowers among the ribbon loops.

3 Snip off half of the "stem" of the pearl-head corsage pins. Secure a small bead to each pin. Apply liquid adhesive to each pin, and insert one into the center of each blossom.

Perfect for a prom or casual wedding, this jazzy nosegay exhibits a vibrant complementary color harmony, established with enchanting red-violet spray mums. The white-tipped blossoms are arranged among tufts of ribbon, in a variety of widths and yellow and green hues, to achieve the complementary palette.

The daisy-flowered chrysanthemums, which are often considered informal, or casual, flowers, are dressed up with sparkling "gems." In addition, an elegant satin-covered posy holder is chosen to coordinate with the ribbon. The chic posy holders are available in numerous colors and with embellishments including tassels, ribbons, pearls, feathers, rhinestones and more, enabling you to design a custom bouquet for every girl.

Grand Orb

Roses and berries comprise a pomander of lavish proportions.

In line with current trends suggesting more lush and full floral compositions, the traditional pomander is "upsized" from its diminutive form, typically used for flower girls, to a size that is both impacting and beautifully suitable for bridesmaids.

This elegant sphere, created with soft orange 'Mambo' spray roses and sienna-hued 'Terracotta' hybrid tea roses, along with fresh green *Hypericum* and permanent orange berries, incorporates a rich palette. The different sizes of roses as well as the inclusion of some tight buds enhances the visual texture and dimension as do the tucked-in groupings of berries.

When softer colors are needed, look for hybrid tea varieties such as ivory 'La Belle,' mottled pink 'Gelatto,' hot-pink 'Tenga Venga' and the sunny 'Orange Juice.'

1 Poke a hole through a floral-foam sphere with a small wood dowel.

2 Attach a wood pick to a chenille stem to form a "T" shape. Insert the chenille stem through the hole in the foam.

3 Attach a ribbon handle to the chenille stem at the top, and arrange flowers into the floral-foam sphere.

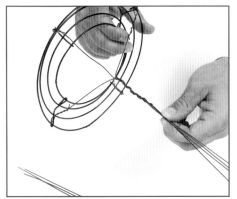

1 Secure four heavy-gauge wires to a wire wreath form in evenly spaced placements. Twist the wires together to form a handle in the center.

2 Disassemble a permanent poinsettia or other foliar material, and glue the leaves on the top and undersides of the wire wreath form in an overlapping manner.

3 Hand-tie a bouquet into the center of the wreath, covering the wire handle.

Leaf-Collared Bouquet

Fabric foliage surrounds a gorgeous bridal bouquet.

Enhancing a resplendent bouquet of fresh roses and permanent berries, a velvet poinsettia plant, in a sundrenched russet hue, is disassembled and repurposed as a leafy collar. The luxuriant foliage is hot-glued onto a wire wreath form, and heavy-gauge wire attached to the form is fashioned into a handle.

The charming blossoms are then hand-tied through the center of the form. Since hand-tied compositions can be dropped into vases for continued hydration before they are used, this design can be made several days in advance and will remain vibrant throughout the nuptial events.

Select foliage in other hues and from other types of faux plants to adapt this technique through every season.

Beaded Blooms

Roses are surrounded by lily grass trimmed with painted beads.

An exquisite offering for nuptials, this dazzling bouquet comprises a stunning hand-tied bundle of 'Freedom' roses. The radiant scarlet blooms are accented by long blades of lily grass (*Liriope*) that are bedecked with painted wooden beads and placed in a starburst fashion around the roses. While the paint color was selected to match the flowers' bold hues, their placement on the grasses suggests a resemblance to seasonal berries.

The lily grass provides a uniform treatment around the stems that gives them an attractive aesthetic no matter from what angle the bouquet is viewed. Similar bouquets also can be dressed appropriately with beads painted to match any of the multitude of rose varieties on the market.

1 Surround a gathering of roses with lily grass. Bind with waterproof tape.

2 Wrap one blade of lily grass around to hide the tape, and tuck it or secure it with a dab of floral adhesive.

3 Slide painted wooden beads onto the blades of lily grass in a random fashion.

1 Dip the handle of a straight-handle bouquet holder into hot-melt (pan) glue, and secure it into a decorative holder.

2 Dip permanent leaves into hot-melt glue, and affix them to the underside of the bouquet holder to conceal its plastic base.

3 Arrange carnations in a lavish mound formation, starting in the center of the bouquet holder and working outward.

Carnation Opulence

Permanent leaves encircle a novel carnation variety.

Using one of the many striking bicolor and novelty varieties of carnations that are available today, this ravishing mono-botanical nosegay demonstrates that the much-maligned blossom has its place at even upscale affairs and is no longer relegated to only the most budget-friendly weddings.

The key is an unusual or unexpected presentation—here, in a radiant mound encircled by permanent *Magnolia* leaves and secured inside a textural posy holder.

This particular variety of carnation, with petals that hint of a creamy green tinged with burgundy, could be encircled with vibrant green foliages as well. Look for this and other novel carnations, and select a fresh or faux leaf to truly showcase the blooms' intriguing color palettes.

Bounteous Bouquet

Textures and colors are highlighted in this magnificent nosegay.

Celebrating fruitful abundance, grand bicolor 'Estelle' roses, in a resplendent terra-cotta hue, are featured along with diminutive *Hypericum* berries, permanent crab apples and fluffy grasses, which, among the large rose blossoms, are most impacting in groups.

Further textural intrigue is added with a soft collar of feather clusters around the bouquet's perimeter. The amazing collection, composed in a bouquet holder, is tailored with an elegant cover, into which the bouquet holder is secured.

Select a decorative cover and floral materials to reflect the seasons. And, while feathers may be appropriate throughout the year, choose those in lighter colors and textures for warm-weather events.

1 Wrap a strip of floral clay around the base of a foam-filled bouquet holder. Secure the holder inside a decorative bouquet cover.

2 Arrange materials into the saturated foam-filled holder. Gather grasses into groups of three or four, and attach steel picks to them. Arrange the grasses among the florals.

3 Tuck feather sprays around the base of the bouquet, forming a soft dimensional collar.

Make-Ahead Bouquet Base

A permanent posy offers a sturdy start to showcase fresh *Freesias*.

Fresh *Freesias* are as gorgeous as they are fragrant, and in this bouquet, in which they're arranged into a base of permanent *Hydrangeas*, they shine brilliantly. The fabric florets, which recede into the background, provide structural support and volume for the fresh flowers, and a contemporary striped ribbon enwrapping the stems accentuates the complementary green and fuchsia hues.

This bouquet's permanent base and its quick-to-construct permanent leaf collar are efficient to arrange ahead of time, especially in multiples for a wedding party. They'll also enable the bouquet to withstand the many demands of a wedding day, such as rough handling, lack of water and temperature fluctuations.

1 Clip permanent *Hydrangea* leaves from their stems. With cool-melt glue, arrange the leaves in an overlapping manner to form a circle with an opening in the center.

2 Group fabric *Hydrangeas*, bind them midway down the stems with waterproof tape and slip the *Hydrangea* cluster into the leafy collar. Arrange *Freesias* into the fabric florals.

3 Secure the leafy collar to the *Hydrangea* and *Freesia* stems with waterproof tape. Finish the handle by wrapping the entire length with ribbon and leaving two decorative tails.

Tabletop Landscape

A horizontally placed wreath graces a variety of tables.

Gardenlike simplicity and beauty are accomplished in this circular vegetative design as long-lasting stars-of-Bethlehem, lilylike *Alstroemerias* and *Nerines*, fragrant hyacinths and exotic lady's slipper orchids rise in dignified groups from a lush base of waxflowers, foliages and reindeer moss.

The range of green and white hues in this composition forms a modern color scheme, which contributes to the design's naturalness, as does the clustered arrangement of the florals. They're placed in a vertical parallel style that reflects how they might grow in a garden. Together, the design style and color harmony give this wreath a peaceful quality that will be welcomed by those who view it in home or office locations.

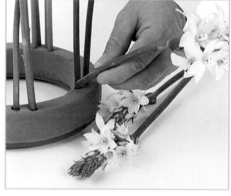

1 Arrange the line flowers vertically in groupings into the floral foam wreath. Fill in at the base with the other materials.

2 Place the stems of the lady's slipper orchids into water tubes, and insert the tubes into the wreath form.

3 Bend wires into hair-pin forms, and secure moss to the wreath base with them, to cover any bare spots.

1 Secure a pillar candle into a vase with floral clay.

2 Place the vase into the center of the design ring, and press the vase down into the foam.

3 Arrange salal leaves and orchids into the foam ring. Bind the orchid stems to wired wood picks for easier insertion.

Center of Attention

Turn a classic candle ring into a safe and stylish centerpiece.

This fresh version of a traditional candle ring incorporates an affordable vase, creating a striking hurricane centerpiece suitable for meeting all types of décor needs, both indoors and out.

Although candle rings are commonly used in homes, this modification is perfect for weddings and parties. In addition to adding value to the arrangement, the vase acts as a safety precaution around the candle flame, so the centerpiece is more conducive to use at outdoor events.

The wreath, composed of salal leaves and green, pink and orange miniature *Cymbidium* orchids, achieves an elegant, tropical appearance that would work well for a function with an exotic theme.

Candle Romance

Special touches enhance this fragrant floral candle ring.

Floral arrangements in a traditional aesthetic are likely to have the broadest appeal, but by employing your creativity, you can add one-of-a-kind touches to your creations. Here, a lush rose and *Freesia* candle ring is enhanced with special accents, enabling it to capture the fancy of brides, party planners and more.

The ravishing red roses are softened by both blush and medium pinks, which are visible in the roses and *Freesias*. Red rose petals are tucked loosely into the center to hide the wreath form, and pussy-willow branches are woven among the flowers to add dimension and rhythm. Garlands of deciduous huckleberry bundles and rolled rose petals tied with red bullion wire are gently laid atop the ring like a veil and add textural intrigue.

1 Cut both ends of a pussy willow branch at 45-degree angles. Insert one end into the floral foam and the other on the opposite side of the ring. Weave in eight to 10 branches.

2 Cut huckleberry into equal lengths. Pile into small bundles. Tie a bundle with bullion wire. Leave a length of wire, and then tie on another bundle. Continue to form a garland.

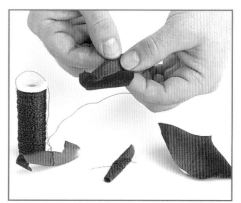

3 Roll a rose petal, following its curve. Gently tie bullion wire around the center of the roll. Leave a length of bullion wire, and repeat the rolling and tying. Continue to form a garland.

1 Arrange *Galax* leaves into the floral-foam wreath at an angle, placing them around its interior and exterior perimeters.

2 Curl pheasant feathers by running the backside of a knife along their spines.

3 Insert the quill of each feather into the foam, arrange it into a curved formation and tuck the tip among Asian honeysuckle vine.

Uncultivated Beauty

Feathers, greenery and vines encircle clusters of roses.

Gatherings of red roses bring refinement to this otherwise rustic, untended-looking wreath. The elegance of the rose blossoms contrasts pleasingly with the wild, sweeping quality of the pheasant feathers and Asian honeysuckle vine, both of which lend a sense of motion to the symbolic composition. *Hypericum* berries and an assortment of foliages, in addition to providing texture, contribute to the wreath's unaffected beauty.

An important element in creating this arrangement is placing the roses at different levels. Securing some farther into the wreath base than others creates depth and draws added attention to the striking red that pops from amid the earth tones.

Wreath Topper

A permanent rose wreath has a new view atop a gardeny vessel.

Whether positioned on doors, on walls or atop moss-enhanced pots such as this one, wreaths are versatile and always in demand. This exquisite example, assembled on a woody vine base and enhanced with gnarled branches, resembles an untended rose garden and can effectively grace tabletops in traditional home and office environments.

Each stem of these grand garden roses, selected in a range of monochromatic reds, represents the luxurious flower's complete life cycle, from tight bud to fully open bloom. The faux stems, assembled with lifelike foliage, are simply woven into the brambly form. Multibranched birch twigs, tucked among the fabric roses, contribute the "wild" aesthetic to the otherwise refined blossoms.

1 Adhere a block of plastic foam inside a clay pot with hot-melt (pan) glue. Dip hyacinth stakes into the glue, and insert them through the upright vine wreath and into the foam.

2 Wrap rose stems around the wreath's vines to secure the blossoms to the wreath. Start at the base and work upward.

3 Clip the tips from several birch branches, and dip the ends into hot-melt glue. Insert the branches between the blossoms and into the wreath base.

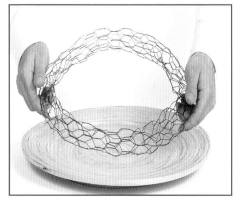

1 Form a 3-foot-long, tubelike structure with floral netting (chicken wire), and shape it into a wreathlike form.

2 Cover the wreath form with sheet moss, and secure the moss to the form with spool wire.

3 Bend the wire stems of permanent flowers into a curved shape, and hot-glue them into the wreath form, all in the same direction.

Cyclone Centerpiece

Tiny fabric flowers appear windswept in this tabletop display.

In the manner of a whirlwind gathering leaves and fragments of debris, this swirl-style wreath design is imbued with a colorful assortment of delicate blossoms intricately woven throughout a circular "thicket" of berried branches.

Rather than being hung on a wall or door, this eye-catching composition is unconventionally placed on a round tray for use as a centerpiece. The base into which all of the permanent materials are arranged is a wreath form made with floral netting and covered with moss.

Practically any materials could be arranged in this fashion, but diminutive blooms, whether fresh or faux, are most suitable for the dynamic motion that is evoked in this whirled wreath.

Front-Door Décor

Prominent placement is required for a lavish fruited wreath.

Few compositions capture the glory of the harvest season like a grand wreath. This one, comprising a vibrant mix of permanent gourds, peppers and berries along with dried quince slices and more, does so with gusto!

To keep the dimensional wreath narrow enough to fit between inner and outer doors, gourds are cut in half and hot-glued to a wooden craft ring. In addition to minimizing the depth of the design, this technique allows the wreath to be completed more cost-effectively than it might seem at first glance. Bits of moss are hot-glued to cover gaps in the base.

Other dimensional materials, such as faux fruits, also could benefit from the hacksaw treatment.

1 Using a hacksaw, cut several large permanent gourds into two equal halves.

2 Glue each of the sliced gourds onto a wooden floral-and-craft ring with hot-melt (pan) glue.

3 Glue additional materials atop the ring. Then, glue bits of moss to conceal the wooden ring and the cut edges.

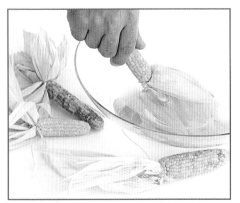

1 Soak husks of miniature Indian corn in warm water. Then shake them, and let them dry.

2 Secure the ears of Indian corn to the *Smilax* wreath base with paper-covered wire. Wrap the wire at the point where the ear meets the husks so that the wire is not visible.

3 Glue the other botanical materials into the wreath with hot-melt (pan) glue.

Aw, Shucks!

Miniature corn and other garden favorites fill a textural wreath.

A golden harvest look is achieved in this abundant wreath, which is composed of dried and preserved materials on a brier *(Smilax)* base. The dramatic range of textures, from smooth pods to fluffy yarrow to bumpy ears of miniature Indian corn, embody a traditional theme — a profusion of garden bounty.

The cream-colored shucks, or husks, of the Indian corn bring an uplifting quality to the palette of golds and russet reds. When purchased, the shucks often will be tightly bound, so soak and shake them to create a fluffier, more captivating look before designing with them.

Look for dried and preserved materials in other color families to create similar stylings throughout the year.

index

5   6   9   10   13   14

17   18   21   22   25   26

29   30   33   34   37   38

41   42   45   46   49   50

53   54   57   58   61   62

65   66   69   70   73   74

77   78   81   82   85   86

89   90   93   94   97   98

101 102 105 106 109 110

113 114 117 118 121 122

125 126 129 130 133 134

137 138 141 142 145 146

149 150 153 154 157 158

161 162 165 166 169 170

173 174 177 178 181 182

185 186 189 190 193 194

197 198 201 202 205

Check out these other inspiring books in
Florists' Review's 101 How-to series:

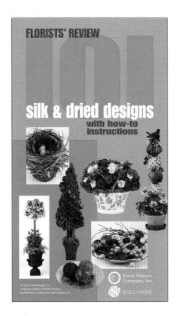

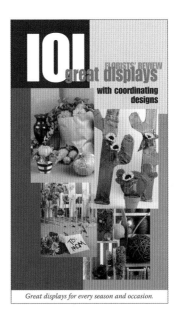